Charitable Status

A practical handbook

Andrew Phillips

Charitable Status
A Practical Handbook
Andrew Phillips

First published in 1980 by InterChange Books, (Then Inter-Action Inprint) 15 Wilkin St, London NW5 3NG
Second edition, October 1982. Reprinted 1984.
Third edition, December 1988.
Fourth edition published 1994 by the Directory of Social Change, Radius Works, Back Lane, London NW3 1HL.

ISBN 1 873860 14 5

The Directory of Social Change is a registered charity, no: 800517.

British Library Cataloguing in Publication Data
A catalogue record for this book is available from the British Library.

Illustrated by Jill Fenwick.
Typeset by Tony Goodman
Printed in Britain by Page Bros, Norwich.

Contents

Andrew Phillips is senior partner of Bates, Wells and Braithwaite, a firm of solicitors which he set up in 1970 in the City of London. He is also a freelance writer and broadcaster, well known for his eighteen year stint as Legal Eagle on the Jimmy Young show (which continues). He was co-founder of the Legal Action Group (LAG) and founder (and still Chairman) of The Citizenship Foundation. His main field of professional activity has for long been advising charities, in which his firm is a leader.

Acknowledgments

In the first edition acknowledgment for the help of a large number of individuals - particularly from among Charity Commision staff - was made.

For this edition I most have to thank my colleagues, Stephen Lloyd, Fiona Middleton and Rosamund Smith for their help.

Lastly, although Keith Smith's crucial involvement in the original editions was not available for this one, his original input is still very much apparent. To my publishers at the Directory of Social Change, and Luke Fitzherbert, my thanks are also due.

Richard Fries has followed one of his predecessors, Denis Peach, in providing a foreword, for which I am grateful.

Andrew Phillips
Spring 1994

The charity label is useful in the hunt for funds

Foreword

The need for a new edition of this practical handbook gives me the welcome opportunity to follow in the footsteps of my distinguished predecessor Denis Peach in providing a foreword to it.

Careful preparation in establishing charities is essential. The Charity Commission has sought to ease the path of those seeking registration for new charities through the guidance material we have published and the model constitutions we have prepared. A proper understanding of the nature of charity and the objects and activities which charity law permits greatly helps the process of setting up a charity on the right lines and in keeping it there.

Richard Fries
Chief Charity Commissioner

Preface to the Fourth Edition

Charitable Status

Since the last edition Parliament has legislated the Charities Act 1992. That in turn, has been partly replaced by the Charities Act 1993, which has consolidated the Charities Act 1960.

Although the 1992 Bill was not politically contentious, the anxieties concerning the bureaucratisation of the voluntary sector - particularly where smaller charities are concerned - are being woefully realised. In addition to the hundred pages of primary legislation, there will be as much again when (not before the end of 1994) all the subsidiary legislation is in place.

To all that must be added further spin-offs, such as the voluminous Statement of Recommended Practice (SORP 2) for charity accounts.

Then there is the European Community, apparently intent on spreading its tentacles to the not-for-profit sector, which in any event is trapped in the maze of Directives and Regulations which can complicate such innocent pleasures as making teddy bears for a charity bazaar or running an 'at home' lunch for funds for the local church.

Against all that, in September 1993 the Prime Minister established an 8th DTI Deregulation Task Force for the Voluntary Sector, charged with rooting out unnecessary complications. With Tessa Baring as its deft Chair, the Charity Commission, the Voluntary Services Unit of the Home Office and a cross-section of the sector (of which I have been the lawyer representative) have surprised themselves by the extent of the agreement. At the time of going to press we are still happily hacking back the regulatory undergrowth.

Recession not withstanding, the vigour and variety of effort by charities large and small never ceases to amaze and delight.

Indeed, in the last 18 months my appreciation of the marvels (and marvels they are) of the British charity sector have been put into sharper focus by visits to Russia, Hungary and Lithuania, helping them to rebuild their shattered voluntary sectors. How fortunate we are (and good luck to them).

If this handbook can help lighten the load of those - particularly the volunteers - who run or aspire to run charities, I shall have been well rewarded.

Andrew Phillips
Spring 1994

1.

Why become a charity?

There are well over a quarter of a million charities, of which about 170,357 are registered with the Charity Commission. This number is steadily increasing by around 4,000 a year. Most charities start small but, like acorns, can and do grow into mighty household names. Others never achieve a single massive shape, but exist as a federation of local, separately registered charities, as is the case with such as the Citizens Advice Bureaux and (by contrast) the Womens' Institutes.

But why do people go to the considerable trouble and (usually) expense of seeking charitable status?

The major advantages

Fundraising & helpers

The public will be greatly reassured if you are a registered charity. Despite the tiny number of highly publicised fraudsters, the word 'charity' still evokes a very positive response in most people. So, although you may not envisage shaking collecting tins on street corners, you may well want to appeal to the public in some other way. "We are a registered charity ..." is an essential label for that.

But sometimes no less important are requests made to grant-giving bodies, most of which are charitable foundations. They, like the public, are bombarded with requests for grants. A few may be prevented by the terms of their constitutions from making grants other than to charitable organisations, but many more are inclined to operate an internal rule of thumb, cutting out all applicants which are not charities. This first winnowing may be crude, but it is a fact of life.

Although there is a steady increase in the numbers of paid staff in the charity sector, the vast majority of helpers are still volunteers. They represent the essence of what the public perceives as 'charitable', and undertake a multitude of functions for the charities they support, from acting as trustees (over a million) to washing up at the village fete (often both!). Without charitable status it will generally be more difficult to attract the necessary volunteers.

Tax advantages

The tax advantages for charities have become increasingly valuable in recent years. Important new exemptions have been introduced. Donors, while receiving no direct financial benefit, often get satisfaction from effectively diverting tax from the State to the charity or charities of their choice. Britain is now probably the most generous tax regime in the world as regards charities and relieves the following:-

- Income Tax - on personal taxable incomes (covenanted, payroll and Gift Aid)
- Corporation Tax on company profits
- Stamp Duty - on the value of property transferred
- Rates - on property rateable values
- Inheritance Tax (formerly Capital Transfer Tax) - on gifts on death
- Capital Gains Tax - on capital profits on asset disposals
- Value Added Tax - on sales of a limited range of goods and services

The taxation system is nonetheless complex and has been changing rapidly in recent years. Details of the above tax reliefs are given in Chapter 11.

The main disadvantages of becoming a charity

Probably the most frequently experienced drawback for an organisation registering as a charity is the limitation the law then places on certain forms of political and campaigning activities. If you expect this restriction to interfere with your activities, read Chapter 9.

Further, the law regulating charities is severe in some respects and has grown far more bureaucratic and intrusive by dint of the Charities Act 1992, part I of which has now been re-enacted, so as to incorporate the Charities Act 1960, as the Charities Act 1993. 100 sections and 10 Schedules long, with a plethora of subsidiary legislation under its terms still to come, the 1993 Act represents a massive increase in regulation.

In particular, the obligations on charity trustees (by whatever name called) are now more extensive and can, in severe cases, carry criminal penalties and/or personal liability for breach of them. This is discussed in chapter 8. As some counterweight to that, charities can now take out indemnity insurance for their trustees (see p73). Lastly, a charity which is in corporate form must comply with the Companies Act as well as charity law.

2.

Forming a charity

Using solicitors

When?

The tradition, as one can call it, in the British charity sector for charities to 'do their own thing' as far as possible is an admirable one. Lawyers and accountants are expensive animals, and only a handful have substantial experience of charity problems.

Nonetheless there is a time to seek the advice of the expert, just as there is a time to paddle one's own canoe. Sometimes a charity actually wastes scarce resources by not getting timely advice.

Who?

When you decide to use a solicitor, try to find one who is reasonably experienced in handling charity formations of the kind you are involved with. Seek recommendations from informed sources - other charities in the same field; grant giving foundations; advisory services and (perhaps best of all) from solicitors you may know.

Cost?

The first thing you will need to establish in going to a solicitor is what he or she can do for you and at roughly what cost. The tendency of many organisations is to skimp setting-up costs, if only because until they are registered they are likely to be extremely short of funds. However, this can well prove to be a false economy. Not only will the inexperienced solicitor tend to give inexperienced advice, but the time it can take to obtain registration can far outweigh any cost advantage. Indeed if a less conventional charity fluffs its application for registration, it will make a second attempt much more difficult, expensive and time-consuming.

A word of warning about costs: the current fashion is to charge according to hourly rates. This can be wildly misleading. The able solicitor with wide experience may quote a higher hourly rate (if he or she is willing to quote one at all), but end up being both cheaper and better. Lastly, observe the thickness of the carpet pile, and the plenitude of marble - clients pay for these one way or another!

Non-cost considerations

At your first meeting with solicitors, you should also find out what experience they have of work of the kind you are asking them to do, and whether they see problems in getting registered. Are they, for example, going to use model 'objects' clauses and other model parts of constitutions already approved by the Charity Commission or the Inland Revenue in some other case?

What priority can they give your work and roughly how long they expect each stage of the formation and registration to take?

You may want to do part of the work involved in formation yourself. Ask if that makes sense. However, to go to solicitors with your own attempts at a draft constitution and require them to work from that usually takes longer and costs more than letting them do things their way.

Crucially, you will need astute advice on the appropriate constitutional arrangements for your charity, particularly if it is a membership or federal organisation. This can be difficult and time consuming, as is reducing the finally agreed arrangements to a clear, well organised format.

How?

The important thing is to instruct a solicitor in whom you have confidence and with whom you can get along. Try to trust him or her to do a reasonable job in a fair way. Most solicitors respond much better to this sort of relationship than one which is over-regulated by the client.

If you have a query or complaint, get it off your chest in a civil way, don't let things fester.

Even if it seems appropriate for you simply to take over another charity's constitution lock, stock and barrel, it may still be advantageous to work with and through a solicitor. Prospects with the Charity Commission are often better if the application and correspondence is routed through a solicitor in non-standard cases.

Other assistance

There are several agencies that are experienced in advising groups how to register such as the National Council for Voluntary Organisations (NCVO), the Civic Trust and the National Federation of Housing Associations. Several of them are described under the Appendix, Useful Organisations. Others may be active in your particular field, so enquire.

What you should do, in any event, is to obtain from another charity in your field, operating as nearly as possible the way you think you would like to operate, a copy of its constitution. This can serve as a guide to you and your solicitor or adviser. If that is not possible, you always have the right to search the public files of the Charity Commission.

These contain constitutions, or 'governing instruments' as the Charity Commission call them, and are indexed alphabetically and by area and type of charity.

What is charitable?

It is not enough for applicants for charitable status to want to do things they consider worthwhile. To be entitled to charitable status there is a legal definition you must come within. It derives, (mirabile dictu), from the preamble to an Elizabethan Act of Parliament of 1601 (since repealed!), redefined in 1891 under four heads by the celebrated judge, Lord McNaghten. To be registered as a charity you will have to satisfy the Charity Commission and Inland Revenue in England and Wales, or the Inland Revenue in Scotland and Northern Ireland, that the purposes or objects of your organisation fall entirely under one or more of those four heads.

The four charitable heads:

(1) the relief of poverty (page 13)
(2) the advancement of education (page 15)
(3) the promotion of religion (page 17)
(4) other purposes beneficial to the community in a way recognised as charitable (page 18)

Objects or purposes clause

The goals for which any charity exists are set out in what is called the objects or purposes clause in its constitution. The objects clause is the foundation stone of the charity, which can do nothing lawfully that does not come within its limits. Anything beyond those limits will be unauthorised or, as lawyers say, ultra vires. If trustees of a charity make gifts or expenditures ultra vires they may well be personally liable to make full recompense to it. (see p71).

Above all, the objects must fall entirely within one or more of the four charitable categories in order for registration as a charity to be obtained and retained.

The first charitable category - The relief of the poor, the sick, the handicapped, the aged and the impotent

There is no neat definition of poverty, but this head extends to the poor, the sick, the handicapped, the aged and the impotent.

The meaning of 'poverty' in its charitable sense is both relative and generous. All those in receipt of State means-tested benefits are almost certain to be charitably 'poor'. But so, too, may be individuals who would certainly not qualify for State support but who, relative to their normal lifestyles and expectations, have fallen on hard times.

Poverty charities can be restricted in benefit

Charities registered under the other three heads must provide benefit to the public at large, or a substantial section of the community. Poverty charities, by contrast, are allowed charitable status even if they only exist to benefit a small group of connected people (e.g. poor ex-employees of one firm). Compare this with an organisation set up to advance the education of the employees and ex-employees of a specified firm (second category) which would not qualify as charitable.

Aged, sick or impotent

The first category also covers relief of the 'impotent' and the 'aged'. The word impotent is nowadays usually taken to mean the sick, handicapped or mentally ill. Modern case law is to the effect that the impotent and aged beneficiaries need not also be poor (though in that event the charity will have to potentially benefit a substantial section of the public).

Thus, in a recent case, provision of housing specially designed for elderly people not necessarily of limited means was held to be charitable.

Relief can be indirect

It is also enough for the relief of poverty to be achieved by indirect means. This might be by providing travel facilities to enable hard-up relatives of prisoners to visit them. Or it could mean the provision of basic equipment or expertise whereby 'poor' people might be enabled to rise above their poverty or create employment for themselves. (E.g. starting up 'soft' loans or grants for unemployed people.)

Poverty charities can have generalised objects

Generally speaking the drafting of objects for this type of charity can be very straightforward, and the Commissioners are usually content with extremely generalised wording.

Example of 'relief of poverty' objects clause

In the past, the courts have accepted under the poverty category such generalised beneficiaries as persons of moderate or limited means or those who are not self-supporting, or poor struggling youths of merit, or debtors or indigent single people. A simple object such as 'the relief of poverty anywhere in the world' is also acceptable and perhaps the best catch-all.

See the Appendix, Further Reading.

Whereby 'poor' people might be enabled to rise above this position and create employment for themselves

The second category - The advancement of education

This is a widely interpreted and dynamic category. As with 'poverty' there is no hard and fast definition. So long as an intelligent and responsible case can be made out to the Commissioners, new branches of teaching, learning and research should find acceptance for charitable status.

'Education' is fortunately interpreted widely and not confined to conventional academic teaching. The promotion of business education has long been looked upon as charitable (so as long as it is not in effect bespoke advice or consultancy), as has the teaching of technical skills.

Sporting facilities and teaching aids are charitable

The definition of education in a charitable sense extends to the promotion of physical education, such as the provision of sports equipment and facilities. Thus, whilst at present a local amateur village football club will not be given charitable status, the same sport in association with education at any level will be a fit recipient of charitable funding. (But see page 28).

Provision of facilities which enable teaching to be more effective such as computers, books, projectors and the running of courses of all sorts are also charitable.

Education in culture and the arts

Aesthetic education in culture and the arts is an expanding field within the education category. The law takes a liberal view of what is permissible in this area, and with careful preparation you should not experience too much difficulty in establishing a charity for the promotion of aesthetic education. For example a choir was registered with objects 'to promote the practice and performance of choral works' and organisations for staging concerts and drama have been registered. Zoos, libraries and botanical gardens come under this head.

Community arts organisations such as street theatre troupes are acceptable to the Charity Commission provided that they are not politically propagandist.

However, 'mere entertainment' or 'artistic purposes' have been held by the courts to be too wide and vague to found a charitable bequest, whereas organisations seeking registration with 'cultural' or 'classical' objects have proved acceptable. These distinctions are bemusing and can only be understood (if at all) in context and in the light of the patchy evolution in case law, inhibited as it is by an inadequate and unschematic flow of cases to the High Court for judicial review.

Education and public benefit

Charitable education need not be restricted to the poor. Eton, after all, is a charity school. But the possibility of benefit to the community or a substantial section of it is essential.

Research

Research activities are generally charitable although, again, they must be of public benefit. In practice this test is usually satisfied by placing the trustees under a duty to disseminate the results of the research by teaching or publication or, at least, to make the research available to the public on a come-and-get-it basis. Thus a research organisation which did most of its work on a sponsored basis which precluded such publication would fail the public benefit test. This is why trade research foundations are generally unsuccessful in obtaining registration, because their benefits are confined to members.

That is not to deny the sponsor and/or charity the right to patent the patentable outcome of such research, and a reasonable delay in publication to accommodate this (six months to a year) would not invalidate the charitable nature of the research.

'Beneficial' Education

Occasionally one must confront the argument that a particular organisation in the education field is not entitled to charitable status because its work, although available to the public, is not 'beneficial'. Thus, to take an extreme case, the courts would not accept as charitable an organisation to educate the young in pornography. 'Teaching' or 'education' has on occasion been distinguished by judges from a simple 'increase of knowledge'.

A case falling the wrong side of this line concerned the provision in the will of George Bernard Shaw for the development of a new alphabet. It was considered so eccentric as to lack the necessary element of benefit. Another case in 1967 involved a 'museum' gift which failed because it had no educational or other real public benefit. The collection amounted, in the words of the judge, to no more then 'foisting on the public a mass of junk'.

Political education

The courts have objected to organisations which propose to operate, or in fact operate, as the propaganda arms of related political groups or parties. By contrast, it has long been accepted that education about politics in an academic way is acceptable, as is education in political principles.

In practice, success or failure in an application for registration on the edge of politics may depend to a great extent on the confidence which the Charity Commissioners have in the applicants and their preparatory work. For further discussion of politics and charity law see Chapter 9. (Also see 'Think tanks' p77.)

An 'advancement of education' objects clause

A simple modern constitution to establish a charity which could operate generally in the education field might have an objects clause as follows: 'To advance education in the United Kingdom for the public benefit.'

However, the Charity Commission tend to dislike such wide objects and would probably seek to narrow them down. But if you reasonably insist that your potential activities may in the future extend to a wide range of education activities, you are entitled to be registered with such embracing objects.

By contrast, the objects of the local playgroup where the sponsors have no wider ambitions would adequately be defined as: 'To provide educational facilities for under-sixes in the town of Charityville'.

The third category - The promotion of religion

'Religion' is not confined to Christian sects

'Religion' includes any form of monotheistic religion though mainstream religions will have an easier passage in registering. The so called non-religious or ethical societies based on humanism are not deemed religious charities but may possibly be eligible for registration as either educational charities or as charities established for other purposes beneficial to the community.

The Church of the Unification (or the Moonies as they are popularly known) were registered by the Charity Commissioners on the grounds that it was not their role to try and evaluate the relative merits of a new religion as compared with an established one. Public outcry against the Moonies' perceived (or perhaps assumed) practices, however, led to a rare appeal by the Attorney General against the Commission in the High Court to have the registration withdrawn. That appeal was not proceeded with for want of evidence, and the registration stands. Mumblings of discontent with this 'undiscriminating' approach invariably founder on devising a reform which is not more unsatisfactory than the status quo.

There must be an outgoing benefit to the public

In a case in 1949 the court decided that a gift for an order of enclosed, contemplative nuns was not charitable because, although plainly a religious gift, the order lacked that outgoing element of advancement (i.e. instruction or edification of the public) which is essential. In reaching this decision the court refused to accept the efficacy to the public of the intercessory prayers of the nuns.

Example of 'promotion of religion' objects clause

On the basis of a Christian charity the objects clause at its simplest might read as follows: 'To propagate the Christian faith for the benefit of the public anywhere in the world'.

The fourth category - Other purposes beneficial to the community

The 'other purposes' are those outside poverty, education and religion but within the so called 'spirit and intendment' of the 1601 Preamble. However, before anyone should think that this offers a bandwagon for all good causes, it is fair to point out that 'other purposes' are not 'all other purposes', but only those beneficial to the community (or a substantial part of it) in a way which is recognised as charitable by law (which is, of course, virtually a circular definition!) Thus, the fourth category is by no means as wide as might first appear.

However, it does give some elbow room in which to extend charitable frontiers and this category perhaps has a more dynamic potential than the others, though all of them have a degree of elasticity, given imaginative advocates, in-touch judges or (more practically) an aware Charity Commission. This organic growth is, after all, the justification for sticking to our case by case (or Common Law) definition of charity.

Community benefit - some examples

In the most general terms this category includes objects of 'general public utility' such as the protection of lives or of the property of the community; preservation of public order; resettlement and rehabilitation of servicemen or offenders; disaster funds; public relief from taxes or rates; general promotion of industry, commerce and art; promotion of public recreation; national or local defence; promotion of moral welfare.

Animal charities fall under this head provided that their objects can be said to benefit the human public, for instance by protecting public morality through prevention of cruelty to animals.

Many of these objects overlap one or other of the three categories already mentioned (e.g. disaster funds as part of the relief of poverty category), thus giving applicants for charitable status two or more strings to their bow.

The provision of recreational and leisure facilities

The Recreational Charities Act 1958 lays down that it is charitable 'to provide, or assist in the provision of, facilities for recreation or other leisure-time occupation, if the facilities are provided in the interests of social welfare'.

However, the registration of amateur sports groups or clubs as charities is still problematic, the law being badly in need of general review and clarification by the courts. Sport

Animal charities are only charitable on the basis of protecting public morality.

as the courts have described it) for 'mere entertainment' or on a private or unduly selective basis is generally not considered to be charitable. Details are given on page 26-7.

Examples of a fourth head, or 'other purposes', objects clause

There is no conventional objects clause for this fourth category of charities, since it is of such wide-ranging scope. However, the Charity Commissioners will, in suitable cases, allow objects stated simply in terms of being 'to relieve poverty, advance education, promote religion and to do all such other things beneficial to the community as may be charitable under the laws of England and Wales' or even 'for the general benefit of the inhabitants of Charityville'.

'Public Benefit' generally

Every charity, other than some poverty charities (see page 13), must be capable of benefiting the whole community or a substantial section of it. As with many other of the tests, it is sometimes difficult to know just how to fulfil this requirement. But it is clear, for example, that clubs are unlikely to be charitable unless the only membership restriction is function related (e.g. promotion of dramatic arts) or a geographical one such as 'for the inhabitants of Charityville'. (e.g. Womens' Institutes are charities.)

It is also clear that 'substantial' in this context can be qualitative or quantitative. For example, a charitable trust to advance education in an obscure branch of physics would not be ruled out because there were only a handful of potential students. On the other hand, an appeal for a single individual - for medical treatment perhaps - cannot be a charitable one, though there may be other ways in which the same effect could be properly achieved.

It is now usually acceptable for a charity in one or other of the four categories to give as its objects the benefit of a foreign public.

Exclusively charitable

A charity can only be registered as such if its objects are exclusively charitable. That is to say all its purposes must be entirely charitable on any sensible reading of the words used. Occasionally this gives rise to difficulties. So it is safer when drafting the objects to link descriptive adjectives by the word 'and' as opposed to the word 'or' so as to require a conjunctive rather than a disjunctive construction.

The importance of drafting objects was vividly illustrated by a case in 1885. There the court, held that 'charitable and deserving' objects were exclusively charitable although, had the words been 'charitable or deserving' they would not have been. For although what is 'charitable', must also be 'deserving', the reverse is not necessarily so.

This does not, of course, prevent you drawing up objects which refer to several heads of charity. In fact it is a positive advantage to do so if you want to have the freedom to be flexible in an evolving world. For example, many Citizens Advice Bureaux have the following simple objects clause:

> *The Bureau is established for the purpose of benefiting the community in Charityville and surrounding area (a) by advancing the education of the public in matters relating to mental, physical and social welfare (b) by relieving poverty.*

It often makes sense to have catch-all objects ('to relieve poverty, advance education, promote religion anywhere in the world and to do all such other things as may be charitably beneficial to the community') and then, without diminishing their generality, to particularise the area in which the charity will expect initially to concentrate its resources.

3.

Types of charity

The following sections describe current law and practice as they affect some types of modern charity.

Self-help

Perhaps the most common form of mutual self-help groups are those established by and for the sufferers from a disability, and those established for health care. Alcoholics Anonymous is one of the best-known groups of this type. If such groups were set up and run by a closed group of people merely for their own benefit they would not be charitable however worthy their aims. But they will qualify if their activities as well as their objects are genuinely for the public benefit by being available to all those within the area of benefit who are suffering from the disability. For example, AIDS sufferers and helpers have set up comparable charities, as have those caring voluntarily for sick and housebound people.

The essential attribute for such a charity is that its membership is open to all within the beneficiary class, with exclusion, or expulsion, only being for good cause (such as refusal or failure to pay a reasonable membership subscription, or conduct damaging to the group's charitable work).

For other types of self-help groups such as local conservation, neighbourhood and community associations, model charitable constitutions exist which provide for a substantial degree of local control.

Models are available from organisations such as the Scottish Council for Voluntary Organisations, Community Matters and for conservation bodies from the Civic Trust (see the Appendix, Useful Organisations).

Support charities - 'Friends' and the like

With the 'opt-out' of state secondary schools from control by Local Education Authorities into grant maintained status, a considerable impetus has been given to the creation and conversion of Parent Teacher Associations (PTAs) and the like into charities to support their respective schools. Similarly, colleges, cathedrals, local museums and buildings of note - themselves charities - increasingly spawn separate support charities (often called 'Friends of' this or that) to aid and abet their work, particularly by fundraising. That is not strictly necessary, because in most cases such 'Friends' can be established under the wing - i.e. within the existing constitutional framework - of the charity supported. However, the internal 'politics' sometimes favour separate organisations. Despite the extra administrative expense of separateness, it can often 'pay off' in terms of motivating the supporters to make a success of what they will feel to be "their show".

Housing associations

Certain housing associations are also acceptable in principle for charitable status. Most now register under the Industrial and Provident Societies Act. The National Federation of Housing Associations (NFHA) has agreed several sets of model rules with the Registrar of Friendly Societies. One set (Model H 1991) establishes an association with charitable status. The NFHA describes this model as 'suitable for associations formed by social, religious and similar groups for the provision of accommodation for persons in necessitous circumstances, e.g. the relief of poverty, general family housing among the lower income groups, as well as the elderly and the disabled'. Further information and advice are available from the NFHA. Note that provision of special housing for the elderly is charitable of itself, there being no compulsory requirement of poverty (see page 13).

Advice giving

If you can clearly show that the advice to be given is educational and/or will be instrumental in relieving poverty and/or distress, registration will be obtained. Some law centres, for example, have registered with objects which include 'to relieve poverty by providing free legal advice and assistance to persons resident in Charityville...'.

The Charity Commission can become anxious where such advice services are available to the well-off. This should not prevent registration, however, where the advice to be given is in furtherance of a plainly charitable purpose - e.g. advice about prevention of unlawful behaviour in relation to an environmental charity. Nor will a charity be prevented from freely educating the public at large in relation to the subject matter of its purposes. Means-testing is then unnecessary, as it is where the general nature of the advice being given implicitly excludes those who are not 'poor', such as on welfare matters.

Distress etc

Although the Charity Commissioners do not like words such as 'distress' to describe charitable purposes, because they are difficult to define, they have accepted that organisations such as the Samaritans and, more recently the Gay London Switchboard, which relieve 'suffering and distress', are properly charitable.

Unconventional medicine and therapy groups

In 1975 the Charity Commission decided that institutions promoting unconventional medicine or therapy would have to satisfy them that the treatments had some merit. That is less likely now with regard to reputable institutions practising activities such as acupuncture, osteopathy or faith-healing but will be required from those practising less well-known forms of treatment.

Evidence could take the form of case studies (possibly from abroad) or indications that the treatment or therapy is acceptable to at least a sector of the mainstream 'medical profession'.

Ethnic organisations/race relations

Bona fide groups set up to relieve poverty, advance education or pursue other charitable purposes among people of a certain ethnic group such as Jews, Irish or West Indians are not discriminatory and can obtain charitable status provided those benefits are not restricted by reference to colour as such. An acceptable phrase to describe, for example, second generation immigrants is 'people of West Indian ethnic origin'. Many such community-type charities are being established these days.

It took many years for promotion of good race relations to be accepted by the Charity Commission, and even longer for the Inland Revenue to agree. If you define objectives in terms of 'the advancement of education in good citizenship' this should be acceptable to the Charity Commission.

If you require further advice on registering a race relations or ethnic group you can contact the Legal Department of the Commission for Racial Equality (See Appendix, Useful Organisations). Local Community Relations Councils are invariably registered as charitable, and their objects are a useful source of ideas.

Employment projects - Training and support

Training for the relief of unemployment has been charitable since 'support, aid and help of young tradesmen, handicraftsmen and persons decayed' was so designated in 1601. But there is an important distinction between providing job training (i.e. education) and providing employment as such. The former is charitable; the second may well not be. Here is an example of such an educational charity registered with these objects:

> *"To further the education and training of unemployed persons, and in particular young persons, by providing them with opportunities for work in the field of social and community service, and by arranging educational courses for them.*
>
> *To relieve need among such persons by providing them with paid employment".*

The major difficulty which arises for some job creation projects is that if they can provide both training and employment, the claim can be made that their purposes are not exclusively charitable and therefore that they cannot register as charitable.

The Charity Commission may look to the rate of turnover of trainees when determining whether the purposes of the organisation are really the provision of training (charitable) or in fact the provision of employment (usually not). Where, for example, there is a turnover of trainees at least every two years the support will generally be viewed as educational. Another long-shot may be to show that your organisation is promoting the development of industry or commerce in general, which is a charitable purpose under the fourth head. A third possibility is to split your operation into two parts so as to hive off the non-charitable workshop element into a business - perhaps owned by the charity (see Chapter 10). This leaves the training element to operate as an educational charity. Further, the charity can pay the business a training allowance, under carefully controlled circumstances, to complete training on the job if, without that subsidy, there would not be the training opportunity. (Also 'Enterprise Agencies')

Here is another recently registered objects clause:

> *"To educate and train young people and adults over the statutory school leaving age in work and life skills likely to enable them subsequently to find satisfactory employment both by arranging periods of work experience and otherwise and by such means also to relieve poverty...".*

A stumbling block may be that if an unemployed person has independent means, but is still desperately looking for a job, he or she may be held not to fit within this category.

To many there is an air of unreality about these fine distinctions. The nearest to overcoming that problem is perhaps the objects clause of Business in the Community, part of which reads:

> *"...Creating or assisting in the creation of opportunities for employment in areas where involuntary unemployment is causing poverty, hardship and distress or physical or mental ill health...".*

Finally, the Charity Commission allows outright, modest grants to people setting up new businesses. A number of charities, led by the Prince of Wales Trust, have pioneered this form of charitable assistance.

Sporting facilities

Most people tend to think that amateur sports clubs and associations should be entitled to charitable status. However, this is not currently the case.

Where the organisation has restricted membership in terms of either who can become a member or which sport or recreation can be pursued if he or she does, charitable status will not normally be awarded.

Types of charity

Promoting physical, mental and spiritual well-being

The requirement that those who use the facilities shall pay some sort of fee or subscription is not, however, considered a restriction in this sense, unless it is plainly of an amount that is calculated to operate as an effective veto on the participation of all but the well-breeched. Further, a geographical restriction (for example to the local village) is not a problem for charitable status.

The law in this area continues to be in a state of uncertainty, indeed confusion. What seems clear, thanks to the Recreational Charities Act 1958, is that provision of facilities for recreation or other leisure time occupation provided in the interest of social welfare (i.e. improving the conditions of life of those affected) for either the public at large or any disadvantaged group (which might be the old or the young) will be charitable. It is under this heading that village halls, for example, are registered.

A model approved by the Inland Revenue and Charity Commission as charitable reads as follows:

> *"The object of the Association shall be the provision in the interests of social welfare of facilities for recreation and other leisure-time occupations for the inhabitants of Charityville being facilities,*

Charitable Status

(a) of which those persons have need by reason of their youth, age, infirmity or disablement, poverty or social and economic circumstances; and

(b) which will improve the conditions of life for such persons by promoting their physical, mental and spiritual well-being."

In order to show that the facility is a provision in the interests of social welfare and that it will improve the conditions of life, some deprivation must exist. This need be no more than the fact that the facilities do not exist locally.

All amateur sports facilities in connection with education, however, are acceptable for charitable status (see p15).

Generally it is unwise to use the word 'sport' in your constitution. The term 'recreation' is better.

Informal, charismatic and other churches

Most traditional Christian denominations do not need to register with the Charity Commission if they establish a new church or chapel. They are by law exempt from so doing (see 'Exempt Charities'). However, some of the newer churches - for example house churches and charismatic sects - are required to register if they want the advantages which go with it. Many do.

Disaster appeals

Following the confusion that arose over the nature of the Penlee Lifeboat Disaster Fund, the Attorney General issued a Statement on Disaster Appeals. You can obtain copies of this from the Charity Commission, the Attorney General's Office or through your bank, local authority or lawyer. It is helpful.

It is vital that specialist advice be taken in the immediate aftermath of a disaster. (If you need pointing in the right direction, the Charities Aid Foundation or National Council for Voluntary Organisations team will help). This is because the wording of the first appeal (often over the airwaves) may well set the seal on all that follows.

Broadly, you have three choices - a charitable appeal; a non-charitable appeal; or a choice for givers by setting up two appeals - one of each. If you choose this last option you must also make clear to which of the two appeals those contributions will go if the giver (as will often be the case) fails to specify which he or she is intending to benefit.

The decision as to the type of appeal will depend on whether you want its trustees to have unfettered discretion as to how to spend the money (in which case you should plump for the non-charitable fund), or to have a discretion limited by the law of charity.

Types of charity

The main consideration here is that if public sympathy is overwhelming and the appeal attracts a mass response, it may mean that to dispose of all the donations to the injured and bereaved would give them far more than charity law would consider to be 'appropriate to their needs'. This would have been the case with the main Penlee Fund, had it been a charitable fund. That in turn would have meant that a large slice of the donations would have had to be kept back for use for general charitable purposes.

For a charitable appeal, therefore, the Attorney General suggests the following form:

> *'The appeal is to set up a charitable fund to relieve distress caused by the accident/ disaster at*
>
> *on*
>
> *The aim is to use funds to relieve those who may be in need of help (whether now or in the future) as a result of this tragedy in accordance with charity law. Any surplus after their needs have been met will be used for charitable purposes designed:*
>
> *(1) to help those who suffer in similar tragedies;*
>
> *(2) to benefit charities with related purposes;*
>
> *(3) to help the locality."*

For those donors who feel that too much help is no help at all, those conditions will give reassurance.

But for those who feel that no sum is too much for those injured or bereaved, they will want their gifts to go to a non-charitable fund if there is a danger (because of the limited number of potential beneficiaries and/or the likely largeness of public generosity) of 'swamping'.

The trustees of a charitable appeal will have to exercise their discretion in accordance with legal constraints, but that still gives them considerable freedom of action. To prevent this by drawing up watertight guidelines for them to work within is unrealistic not only in terms of the critical timescale which operates in the wake of a disaster, but also because tight guidelines will never be able to deal with all eventualities and can cause worse anomalies than no guidelines at all.

Charitable Status

One red-herring is that of tax. Few if any of the donations given to a non-charitable appeal fund will attract tax either by the giver or by the fund. As regards the former, the inheritance tax free limit for non-charitable annual gifts is £3,000 (limitless for charitable gifts), and each donation to the appeal is looked at separately for tax purposes.

Furthermore, regardless of the disaster funds' status, the Inland Revenue will generally not seek to tax the proceeds of fundraising events, even where they are large-scale and repeated.

That only leaves interest etc. earned on the accumulated fund which is subject to tax if it is a non-charitable appeal. However, given swift administration, that may well be a relatively minor matter. (See Bradford Disaster Fund under Useful Organisations for further information.)

4.

Applying for charitable registration

The Questionnaire

The Charity Commission will not be concerned only with your objects clause. In the long questionnaire which all applicants for charitable status are now required to complete there are a series of questions aimed at eliciting your plans. Your answer to these requires care, and sometimes advice. Where, as is often the case, the promoters of the charity are genuinely uncertain as to the programme its trustees will adopt (usually because either they have not been selected, or have not met), that should be plainly stated. The worst mistake is to set out over-detailed or grandiose plans which, in the event, the charity does not or cannot carry through and which may give rise to needless queries.

Where genuinely appropriate, adopt the objects clause of a registered charity which is engaged in similar activities to your own. If you tell the Charity Commission that you followed such a precedent, or model, it may make your passage to registration quicker and smoother.

It is vital to try and draft your objects clause correctly the first time. This is the moment, then, to obtain expert advice if you are at all unsure of your ground. Although you can re-submit a draft constitution with changed objects after rejection of the first draft by the Commission, this may incline them to think either that you don't know what you are doing, or that you are disguising your real and uncharitable objects behind a charitable facade. (See Objects, p45, also Difficulties in Registration, p32).

Application

It tends to be easier for a group that is still constituting itself to register as a charity than one which is up and running.

Therefore, if you think that it may be to your group's advantage to have charitable status later on, you should consider registering as a charity early, particularly before the press has written about your activities. This and your own publicity material can inadvertently give the Charity Commission a false idea of your real purpose.

If however, you need to establish your organisation before Charity Commission approval has been obtained (for example, to take premises or employ a key person), make sure that the constitution expressly allows any amendment to be made for the purposes of achieving charitable status.

Registration as a charity can take from two weeks or so (in a special emergency) to two years, depending on whether the proposed charity is clearly charitable or has purposes which are borderline. (One group I helped register had been battling for five years before they came to me.)

In the first instance you send your draft constitution (i.e. before you formally adopt it) or your existing constitution (where you are already formed) to the Charity Commission for their comment. If you are located in Scotland or Northern Ireland, send instead to the Charity Division of the Inland Revenue.

You also complete the Charity Commission Questionnaire at this stage. The second registration form is not completed until the end of the approval process.

Consideration of application

In England and Wales the Charity Commission normally satisfy themselves that you are entitled to charitable status, and that the constitution is satisfactorily drafted, before sending it on to the Charity Division of the Inland Revenue (at Bootle) for their views. In the process there may be considerable enquiries and correspondence, and even meetings. A meeting is sometimes the best way of overcoming the Commission's misgivings.

Difficulties in registration

Don't be put off if you get rebuffed at your first approach for registration. Do try and make sure, however, that if you have not already done so at that stage, you take good advice.

Sometimes a meeting with the person dealing with your case at the Commission will help. Sometimes it is better simply to persevere in correspondence, producing fuller facts and more persuasive legal backing to support your application. The Charity

Commission will often suggest how you should change the wording of your draft constitution to satisfy both them and the Inland Revenue. You may well have to drop or alter some of your proposed purposes or powers, but you must take expert advice if you are unsure of the impact of their suggestions. It is ill-advised to 'buy' consent by restricting your objects in a way which could have profoundly serious consequences later.

In your dealings with the Charity Commission be patient and polite. Be well briefed and be flexible. If you are convinced you have a good case, persist. If an application is likely to prove difficult, don't wait until you have been rebuffed to get advice.

Appeals

If, after corresponding with an executive of the Charity Commission over your draft constitution, you think his or her refusal to register your organisation is legally wrong, you can ask for a formal adjudication by the Charity Commissioners sitting as a board.

You will be asked to submit a written reasoned statement of your case, if you have not already done so. The Commission's lawyer does the same. Since this will usually require detailed knowledge of charity law you will need to engage a knowledgeable solicitor, if you haven't already. The Commission's formal adjudication, which does not involve an oral hearing, is free.

If the outcome is not in your favour your next recourse can be an appeal to the Chancery Division of the High Court, thence to the Court of Appeal and finally (with consent) to the House of Lords. Very few organisations appeal to the High Court, for it is an expensive course of action, for which legal aid is not available and in respect of which (contrary to the normal rule) you cannot always recover your costs from the Charity Commission and/or Inland Revenue if you win (but that also works in reverse).

Fees

No fees are currently charged by either the Charity Commission or the Inland Revenue. But bear in mind that you may have substantial solicitors' fees, and will have a registration fee if you incorporate as a company or Industrial and Provident Society (see p45).

It is anticipated that the Commission will in due course charge a registration fee under S.85 of the 1993 Act.

Charitable Status

Scotland

The principles of registration as we have explained them also apply to organisations based in Scotland, except that the Charity Commission's remit does not cover Scotland. Therefore, prospective charities should send their draft constitution and a copy of their latest accounts (if any) to their local Inspector of Taxes. Once this has the Inspector's approval, submit a certified true copy of your constitution, as finally approved, to the Inspector and you should receive a letter from the Inland Revenue in Edinburgh establishing your charitable status and giving you a reference number. There is no register of charities in Scotland.

Advice on charitable registration can be obtained from the Scottish Council for Voluntary Organisations (see Appendix, Useful Organisations).

The Charities Acts only apply to Scottish charities insofar as they are mainly managed or controlled in England or Wales or have property there, but under Part I of the Law Reform (Miscellaneous Provisions) (Scotland) Act 1990 the Inland Revenue keeps a public index of Scottish charities and the Lord Advocate is given power to intervene if mismanagement is suspected.

Northern Ireland

Northern Ireland is similar to Scotland. An organisation based in Northern Ireland wanting charitable status should draw up its draft governing instrument and submit it for clearance to the Charity Division of the Inland Revenue in Bootle (see Appendix, Useful Organisations).

Under the Charities Act (Northern Ireland) 1964 the Charities Branch of the Northern Ireland Department of Finance was given many similar functions (but not registration) to those of the Charity Commission for England and Wales, but with restricted powers. They will, for instance, give advice to charities and prospective charities.

[NB. Northern Ireland charities are exempt from rates.]

The Inland Revenue

During the process of vetting a prospective charity, the Charity Commission automatically consults the Inland Revenue unless the applicant clearly falls within one of the established charitable precedents.

Since the Inland Revenue stand to 'lose' tax revenue each time a new charity is registered, they tend to be tougher on applicants. Sometimes, therefore, the Charity Commission will argue with the Inland Revenue in favour of granting charitable status. The Charity Commission may suggest alterations in draft constitutions to the applicant to overcome objections that have been lodged by the Inland Revenue.

Applicants for charitable status may find themselves in the frustrating position of having to argue with the Inland Revenue at one remove, because their dealings will be exclusively with and through the Charity Commission.

Even after a charity has been registered, the Inland Revenue can and will refuse tax relief if the income of the charity is not in fact 'applied' for charitable purposes. This is dealt with in more detail in Chapter 11. On occasions, however, the two bodies disagree. Since the Charity Commission can place a charity on the register without the agreement of the Inland Revenue, that leaves the latter with the option of challenging the registration in the High Court.

5.

Legal formats

A group with ideas of forming a charity is well-advised sooner rather than later to define exactly what it is they are seeking to achieve, and by what means and programme. In putting together your constitution you should seek:

- clearly but broadly to define the objects/ purposes/ aims/ends of the would-be charity and the possible means of achieving them (i.e. the powers);
- to build in arrangements for the charity's governance likely to foster the good and equitable conduct of its affairs;
- so as to minimise disputes at a later date to provide a framework for the resolution of disputes if and when they do occur;
- to spell out the rights and obligations of the trustees, members, and any committees, branches, advisory council and so on, so that everyone knows where they stand.

It can be difficult to get to speak to the person who...

The choices - corporate or unincorporated

The major options are:

Unincorporated organisations
- (a) Unincorporated association, society or club
- (b) Trust
- (c) Friendly Society

Corporate organisations
- (a) Company
- (b) Industrial and Provident Society
- (c) Royal Charter body

The status of corporate and unincorporated charities compared

The company

The major legal difference between corporate and unincorporated organisations is that a corporate organisation is more than the sum of its parts. It has a legal existence independent of its members. Thus, while it is only able to act through human agents (usually called its directors), the corporation has its own rights and duties.

The implications of this are evident in an unincorporated organisation, which has no separate legal existence, so that any property acquired for its purposes can only be held on its behalf by the (usually individual) trustees.

The company is only born when the Registrar of Companies issues its promoters with a Certificate of Incorporation (which includes its registered name and number). That will only happen after the incorporation formalities have been completed.

The Trust

Trusts - which are a unique flowering of English legal culture - have been used since time immemorial to establish and regulate formal relationships between three parties. The first (the donor) agrees with the second (the trustees) to put into their hands money or property (the trust property) to be used exclusively for its charitable objects (i.e. within the area of benefit, or for its beneficiaries) without personal benefit to the trustees.

The trust relationship, simple in concept, can also be simple to create - word of mouth being technically sufficient. However, the Charity Commissioners, not surprisingly, require written evidence of the existence and nature of the trust in order that they may determine whether it is charitable or not.

The trust is often ideal for simple, or single purpose, charities, small-scale charities and charities not looking to management participation by volunteers or members.

Quick and often relatively cheap to set up, the trust has been the traditional format for charities. The trust constitution, known as the Trust Deed, can be short where its objects are simple, and can be prepared without reference to any outside authority. As a result, no statutory fees or taxes are payable on formation of a trust. As regards saving time and money at the outset, the trust is better than the company. But it is not often that these factors ought to take precedence over all others. Furthermore, if comprehensiveness of constitutional arrangements is important, the company format is clearly superior.

Liability - the trust

The principal disadvantage of the charity established as an unincorporated trust, association, society or club is usually perceived to be the unlimited personal liability to which its governing body (by whatever name called) will be individually exposed. For they will usually be personally liable under contracts entered into on behalf of the charity, and if it is sued their names will appear on the summons or writ and it is they who will ultimately have to pay any damages. Indeed, they are jointly as well as individually (i.e. severally) liable, so that a rich trustee could end up carrying the load for his or her poorer brethren. In that event he or she will have a right of equal contribution from each of them, but that may not be collectible.

Although normally trustees will be entitled to be reimbursed out of the charity's assets, this will be of limited consolation if the charity simply does not have the wherewithal. They then remain liable.

Common examples of liabilities trustees might expect to assume would be in respect of rental payments and repair obligations under a tenancy, or in respect of service or hire purchase payments contracted for by the governing body on behalf of the charity. There is also the (remote ?) prospect of the charity being sued for negligence, or having its financial planning wrecked because of fraud. If it is uninsured, the trustees may well be personally liable for the aftermath.

However, these risks can easily be exaggerated. These days one can get insurance for most things. Bear in mind, too, that the trustees of a charity - whether unincorporated or in corporate form - are not supposed to take financial risks. That is to say, obligations should only be incurred as and when the resources to meet them are either in hand or more or less assured. The law expects the governing body to act prudently.

Further, a trustee will not be personally liable for obligations incurred where it is clear that the trustees were only contracting to the extent of the charity's assets.

Liability - the company

The company format was developed in the last century as a convenient method whereby a disparate group of people could associate together for a common but specific purpose in a convenient, controlled way and with limited personal liability.

Despite that, it is rare indeed to find men and women content to allow their names to be used as trustees who would also be content to walk away from liabilities they have incurred on behalf of their charity to innocent third parties. (Also see 'Liability' p71).

The 'wrongful trading' provisions of the Insolvency Act 1986 will strip trustees/directors of the protection of limited liability if they knew or ought to have known that there was no reasonable prospect of the company avoiding insolvency. This can be a tricky test to apply and professional advice should be taken well before that position is reached.

So, too, the limited liability status of a charity will not protect its directors under charity law against personal liability if they permit it to operate beyond its proper charitable scope or otherwise in breach of their trusts.

This is because the directors of a corporate charity are also its trustees. As such they are subject to the provisions of both the Companies Acts and the charity laws controlling trustees.

[N.B. If a charity which is a company wishes to drop the word 'limited' from its name, that can now be achieved simply by swearing and filing with the Registrar of Companies the necessary statutory declaration.]

The formalities of day-to-day running compared

The informality and flexibility of the unincorporated body, free of the voluminous and unforgiving tentacles of the Companies Act 1985, works well where the charity is for a limited or local purpose, or where it is well blessed with reserves, or is a grant-giving charity, and hence indifferent to liability issues.

Not to have to comply with company law requirements for the holding of meetings, the filing of resolutions, the lodging of annual returns and so on, is a major benefit, especially for unpaid volunteers. The muddle into which very many otherwise well-run corporate charities get themselves in relation to the fine print of company law and their constitutions provides a warning against too enthusiastic a rush to incorporation.

On the other hand, non-incorporation is usually riskier if serious disagreements break out, because then one is left relatively unsupported in terms of a constitutional framework within which to head off, or resolve, the same. At such times the mass of detailed company law provisions which automatically apply can prevent the substantive disagreement being complicated by a host of procedural ones. Contrariwise, if those company law provisions have not been kept pace with, the reverse may be true.

It is not a bad thing to look around and see how other well-run charities of your type organise themselves.

What is clear, and as will be explained in more detail later, is that for the larger, membership charity the corporate form is likely to be the right one. It provides the fulsome regulation, control and certainty which will be needed, plus a worked out constitutional relationship between the trustees/directors and the members.

Few trusts, by contrast, have a class of members separate from the trustees, with all that that can involve. Too often that means that there is no way of removing the idle, ineffective or merely tired trustee.

Constitutional changes compared

Provided that the trust deed was drafted to allow changes in its terms, the speed and ease of effecting the same can be a significant advantage compared to the highly regulated and laborious procedure which is obligatory for companies. However, the Charity Commissioners will not accept for registration any charity whose constitution allows for changes in its charitable objects without their consent, which can be given in very limited circumstances only. To change the Memorandum or Articles of a company, by contrast, is a laborious process, involving initiating the calling of a general meeting, formal notices, a precisely worded special resolution and subsequent filing obligations. Changes to the Memorandum are also vulnerable to subsequent attack by dissident members.

The company

Constitution

The Companies Act 1985 provides a ready-made, comprehensive framework which, tailored to the circumstances of the particular charity, will usually provide for the day-to-day pressures and strains which is the lot of any dynamic, participatory charity. In particular regulations under the Companies Act 1985 provide a Model Constitution, known as Table 'C'. Table 'C' includes detailed provisions for the holding of general and directors meetings; voting rights; altering members rights and the constitution of the company, and a myriad other matters.

The promoters can add or subtract from Table 'C' as, within certain limits upon which a lawyer will advise, they think fit. Normally anyone can be a member if the directors admit them to membership within the constitution. Expulsion powers can also be provided (subject to the principles of natural justice).

However, arrangements vis-a-vis new members and election or appointment of directors can be multifarious, and need experienced advice in unconventional cases.

Participation and accountability

Companies have a two-tier power structure so that although the directors hold day-to-day power, the right of removing them must (by the Companies Act) ultimately rest with the members of the company. In contrast the trustees of a trust normally have no check on their longevity in office other than their consciences and any limitations in the trust deed. Thus, if they regularly fail to use their powers effectively, or even at all, there is usually no practical means of unseating them.

Usually neither the Commissioners nor the courts will interfere on questions as to the quality of the trustees' performance, but only in relation to its legitimacy according to the terms of the trust deed and the general law of trusts. (Trustees should, though, be aware of the extent of their financial liability described in Chapter 8.)

All trusts must have at least two trustees, but there is no maximum limit placed by law on their number. Most charitable trusts appear to have an odd number of trustees ranging from three to nine. An uneven number avoids deadlock (and is less contentious than a casting vote). The trust deed should clearly specify the circumstances in which trustees can be appointed and removed and by whom. For further details see p57.

Charitable Status

The Limited Company - Limited by shares or guarantee?

There are two main types of limited company. The norm in the field of commercial activity is the company limited by shares. This is almost always an unsuitable format for a charity to adopt. The lesser known type of company, appropriate for a charity, is the company limited by guarantee.

In the company limited by shares, liability for the debts of the company is limited to the nominal value of the shares held by the shareholders (its owners). Whereas, in a company limited by guarantee, there being no shareholders, the members agree to guarantee to pay any residual debts of the company up to a limit of (normally) £1 each. This must be specified in the Memorandum.

Companies are now governed by the Companies Act 1985. Company constitutions consist of a Memorandum (containing objects and powers) and Articles of Association (rules and regulations).

Rather than trying to form your own company, you can usually obtain a company from law agents "off-the-peg" or from solicitors "tailor-made". The latter is, obviously, much more expensive in the short run, but is likely to be far better in the long term.

Friendly Societies

Friendly Societies were an invention of the last century when a massive number of these self-help voluntary associations were set up to stave off the terrors of sickness, indigence and misfortune. Today they are of fast declining popularity, with hardly any charitable creations being made.

It is, however, possible to be both a Friendly Society and a charity, in which case the society is exempt from registration with the Charity Commission but must register with the Registry of Friendly Societies under the Friendly Societies

A manufactured legal person

Act 1974 (see Appendix, Useful Organisations). The relatively simple structure, the ease of transferring property and the recourse to fairly cheap arbitration at the Registrar's office in the case of disputes, are advantages of becoming a Friendly Society. While this may appeal to some small charitable groups, such as those concerned with mutual relief of hardship, most decide to go one step further and become incorporated as either a company or an Industrial and Provident Society.

The Industrial and Provident Society

Characteristics

The Registrar of Friendly Societies has the statutory job of overseeing the life and times of Industrial and Provident Societies (IPSs) as well as that of Friendly Societies. His two charges are somewhat different animals. Whereas the unincorporated Friendly Society is in effect a form of partnership of individuals, the IPS is an incorporated organisation, so that it has an identity distinct from its members.

An IPS will be charitable if it fulfils the normal criteria. Although it does not have to register with the Charity Commission, being exempt under the 1993 Act, if you plan to set up a charitable IPS, it is wise to send a draft set of rules to the Charity Division of the Inland Revenue to obtain their guidance on whether they would accept the IPS as charitable for tax purposes. This does not ensure that you will obtain tax relief when you apply, but it is the nearest you can come to gaining advance recognition.

Becoming a charitable IPS is unusual. Applicants, other than housing associations, may find it difficult to satisfy the two sets of requirements - those for being charitable and those for being an IPS.

Charitable Status

An organisation qualifies for registration as an IPS if it is a society for carrying on an industry, business or trade and is either a bona fide co-operative society or is intended to be conducted for the benefit of the community. Only an IPS within the last mentioned category may be charitable. One could imagine an open-membership self-help group of disabled people wanting to provide special training and work for themselves who could satisfy both sets of criteria.

To fall into the category of being for the benefit of the community the society must be non-profit-distributing, that is to say one which prohibits by its rules the distribution of its assets among members. In common with an IPS registered under the co-operative clause, control should be vested in the members equally and only moderate interest can be paid on share or loan capital. Other restrictions apply but they are unlikely to worry an organisation with charitable intent.

Broadly speaking the rules of any organisation registering under the Industrial and Provident Societies Act 1965 have to comply with the list of requirements set out in the First Schedule to the Act, all of which are in any event matters which a prudent group of people would want to sort out in advance. More details are available in form F.617 available from the Registry of Friendly Societies (see Appendix, Useful Organisations.)

IPS and Company compared

Those wanting to establish a corporate charity may wish to compare the IPS format to the limited company format.

The rules and formalities of the IPS are less rigid, complex and onerous than are those for companies. This no doubt relates to the fact that IPSs are not primarily profit-generating organisations, whereas commercial companies are; and charitable companies are not differentiated from mainstream non-charitable companies when it comes to statutory regulation.

An IPS can convert into a limited company if that ever proves to be necessary or desirable. And a company can likewise convert to an IPS. Unless it consists of two or more registered societies an IPS requires at least seven members.

If an IPS registers using model rules submitted through

a 'promoting society' such as the National Federation of Housing Associations, it can be quite quick and cheap to register, for you are unlikely to need a solicitor and the Registry's special fee for applicants using model rules is £200. If you do not use model rules it is necessary to send your draft rules to the Registry for comment before finalising them. This procedure will take much longer and the fee is £535. You will also then need to satisfy the Inland Revenue (the Charity Commission does not register IPS charities) as to charitable status.

By comparison a company can be formed in a few days. However, registration with the Charity Commission generally for a conventional case now takes from three to nine months. The fee for registering a company with the Registrar of Companies is £50 plus the cost of printing, seal, statutory book etc (approx £70 more) and any solicitor's fees.

The contents of your Constitution

Generally

The constitution (which can take the form of a Trust Deed, Association Rules/Memorandum and Articles/or other governing instrument) is to a charity as bricks are to a house. If wrongly put together, the inadequacy can shackle the charity for evermore. It is, therefore, essential that unless you are following a model which really does fit, you should get good advice from someone experienced in drawing up (or drafting) such documents. It really is an expert activity.

These are some of the major matters which the constitution ought to cover:

Objects (or purposes, aims or 'ends')

The most important clause of any constitution is that which defines what the organisation exists to do i.e. its objects or purposes. In drafting the objects it is vital to define them so that if circumstances change, and as the organisation evolves, its new activities will still be within bounds.

It is also important to resist the temptation to draw up your objects clause as a ringing declaration of your ideals. This can sometimes frighten off the Charity Commissioners, who may feel that the organisation sounds over-political or partisan. It is improbable, in any event, that the two statements - legal objects and public appeal - can be satisfactorily accommodated in a single form of words.

It is helpful for trustees to understand that it is entirely up to them as to how the charity operates within its objects. They can ignore 90% of their scope and concentrate all activities within the 10%. No-one can attack them for so doing.

Powers

The constitution should clearly define the powers (or means) by which the objects (or ends) can be promoted. A 'power' is a discretion, and need not be exercised. As with objects, it usually pays to give your trustees/directors maximum room for action, i.e. the widest discretion.

It is worth mentioning that if they are given wide powers, trustees/directors can themselves make internal 'rules' or guidelines for the administration of the charity. They may, for example, specify standing orders for meetings, or rules about use of charity property. Such day-to-day arrangements are not suitable for inclusion in the constitution itself, and can be brought in and phased out simply by trustees'/directors' resolutions.

The trustees/directors should be given power to delegate the exercise of their powers on a wide basis. (See p54).

Some other important, general powers to include are investment, lending and borrowing, employment, insurance (including trustee's liability) acquisition and occupation of property, alteration of the constitution, permissible trade, and the setting up of related companies and charities (see Ch. 8).

Trustees/directors

It is the trustees of the trust, the directors of a company, and the committee of an unincorporated association who have ultimate policy and executive power in a charity. The scope of their authority should be clearly defined, especially if there are other, lesser sources of power (advisory councils, branches, regions etc.) It is essential that you describe how and when they can be removed and new appointments made (see p57).

Members

As we explained earlier, most trusts do not have members as distinct from trustees. However all companies do, as is the case with unincorporated associations. One must define clearly the rights and duties of members, and how new members can be admitted and existing ones removed. It is also essential to stake out precisely the constitutional relationship between members on the one hand and trustees/ directors on the other. Charities should think hard before destroying what can and normally is the creative counter-balance between directors and members by reducing them to exactly the same group of people.

Delegation See page 54

Altering the constitution

To provide against unforeseen circumstances it is important to give power for the constitution to be changed, though you will need to think carefully about the conditions which must be satisfied in the process. The objects clause cannot be changed without the consent of the Charity Commissioners. In the case of a charitable company this is provided by the Charities Act 1993 and in the case of unincorporated charities that is the general law.

Elections

If you are to elect any of the trustees/directors or officers then the mechanics need to be clearly spelt out. For example, do they rotate on fixed terms (e.g. one third retire every three years) or stay put until they resign or are voted out?

One of the advantages of a company is that full (though changeable) provisions are made in the Companies Act, particularly in its model regulations known as Table C.

Investment

It is important to define, and to define widely, the investment powers of the governing body of the charity. (See pages 50 and 55)

Bank accounts

Opening and operating arrangements for bank accounts must also be spelt out clearly. It usually makes sense for the governing body to be able to instruct the bank to accept the signatures of whoever they may choose to operate the accounts of the organisation, even if the signatories are not themselves on the governing body. However, the Charity Commission will normally seek to insist on two trustee signatories, and will be correct in warning that for trustees to leave the signing of cheques entirely to others can in some circumstances constitute negligence which could subject them to personal risk.

Dissolution - the power to dissolve

Whatever form a charity takes, its constitution ought to contain a clause enabling it to be wound up. It is quite common to make an arrangement whereby a special majority (sometimes all) of the trustees, or three-quarters of the members of a charitable company voting on the matter, have the authority to dissolve the charity. In the case of associations, such as charitable community associations, the power may be cast wider.

Surplus assets on dissolutions

It is essential that a dissolution clause states what should be done with any surplus left on dissolution, after all the obligations of the charity have been paid off. The law requires that it should go to another charity, or for charitable purposes. Otherwise monies which have been donated to the charity could find their way to non-charitable causes.

Often the arrangement is that any surplus goes to another charity operating in a similar field chosen by the majority of the trustees. Sometimes that charity is actually named in the dissolution clause. Alternatively discretion is left completely to the trustees to exercise at the time. The following clause is one example:-

> ... the assets of the charity (if any) after payment of all proper debts and liabilities should not be paid or distributed amongst the members but shall be given to such other charitable organisation or organisations with objects similar to those of the charity as the members for the time being shall decide or in default of any such decision within a month of the resolution to dissolve as shall be decided by the committee. (All such decisions to be by simple majority.)

It is emphasised that this wording may not be suitable to your circumstances.

Discontinuance without dissolution

If there is no dissolution clause in the constitution of a charity and no amendment clause enabling one to be inserted, or if the means by which such an insertion can be made or a dissolution clause implemented cannot be triggered (perhaps because unanimity is needed and one trustee is holding out), there is an alternative. This will be for all the assets of the charity to be given away within its objects (having met or made full provision for its liabilities, actual or contingent).

'Merger'

It is increasingly common for charities in the same field to join forces. Rather than dissolving both such charities and creating and registering a new charity to which all the net assets of the wound up charities are transferred, it usually makes sense to select one of them as the continuing vehicle and simply transfer assets from the other charity into it.

That will only be done when the charities have reached comprehensive agreement on the future basis of their 'merged' activities. This will cover such issues as debts and other liabilities, constitutional changes to the continuing vehicle, its governing body, broad future policy and name.

Charity Commission models

Life has been made considerably easier for applicants for charitable status with no special constitutional needs. There are now model constitutions provided by the Charity Commission itself - one for charitable trusts (GD2) and one for charitable companies (GD1) and a third for unincorporated charitable associations (GD3).

The applicant will still have to draft the appropriate charitable purposes, which is the heart and soul of the constitution. Still, where the charity is a conventional one that should be no problem, and already it is clear that the models will be extremely helpful to many applicants.

It is not by any means guaranteed that use of a model will ensure unquestioned and swift grant of charitable status. Each case will have to be considered on its merits, and the Charity Commission will still need to be satisfied as to the objects and the appropriateness of the model to the likely practical needs of the applicant.

The model documents are, at the time of going to press, free and can be obtained by telephoning one or other of the Charity Commission offices (see Appendix, Useful Organisations).

6.

Charity trustees and the running of a charity

Charity trustees

The term 'trustee' can be confusing. All charities must have charity trustees or their equivalent. In the Charities Act 1993 the term is defined as 'the persons having the general control and management of the administration of the charity'. In a company established for charitable purposes, the directors are the equivalent of the charity trustees. In an unincorporated charitable club or association the executive committee (by whatever name called) will fulfil that role. In this chapter we use the term 'trustee' to cover all these types of charity trustee.

Choosing the right trustees for a charity is vital. It can also be a bit baffling. Should you invite friends, or eminent names, or local worthies? What qualities or abilities will the trustees need? Can they be paid? What responsibilities are they taking on?

Responsibilities of trustees

In a nutshell, the trustees of a charity have full control of what the charity does and how well it does it. Their overriding duty is to ensure that the purposes, or objects, of the charity are effectively and properly carried forward as laid down in the constitution of the charity. This means, for example, that they are required to ensure that the funds and assets of the charity are properly invested, administered and used. The Charity Commission issues two free booklets entitled 'Responsibilities of Charity trustees' and 'The Charity Commissioners; how they can help Charity trustees' which set out the bones of this topic. (See p71 for trustees' liability).

Choosing trustees

You will want to balance your trustees and the advantages which each of them will bring to the charity. That will be determined by reference to the nature and level of activity planned for it. Bear in mind that the trustees collectively have the final say on everything. It is far more important that they are likely to prove committed and capable than that they be eminent. Obviously, and in all cases, they need to be absolutely trustworthy.

It is also important to seek to achieve harmony - indeed mutual enjoyment in working together - amongst trustees. They are, after all, volunteers.

The Charity Commission are not usually concerned with the identity of proposed trustees in any direct way. However, they will be comforted by the knowledge that the proposed trustees are people who have a reputation to lose and who, merely by being trustees, show their own confidence in the organisation. This can be particularly helpful where it is unconventional in its aims.

Patrons etc

You should also bear in mind the fundraising importance of having well-known people openly associated with your charity. But since they are, by definition, likely to have many other calls on their time, one can sometimes get the best of both worlds by engaging these 'big names' as 'patrons' (or whatever) rather than trustees. The title 'patron' is a purely honorary one, which does not give them either the power or the responsibility which attaches to a trustee.

Paying trustees and worker trustees

First, if the constitution of a charity as registered makes no provision for trustee remuneration, that cannot subsequently be altered other than with consent of the Charity Commissioners.

The Charity Commission take the view that generally the trustees of a charity should not make any profit out of their position, nor should they be placed in a position where their duties as trustees might conflict with their personal interests. Accordingly, the Commission will generally refuse to register an applicant whose constitution does not prohibit remuneration of trustees. There are exceptions.

The first is in respect of professional trustees, such as solicitors and accountants, where the Commission will allow the constitution to provide for their remuneration in the normal way. It may therefore be wise to include the following clause in your constitution:-

> *"Subject to the approval of the other trustees in any case, any trustee for the time being hereof being a solicitor or other person engaged in any profession shall be entitled to charge and be paid all usual professional or other charges for work done by him or her, or his or her firm, when instructed by his or her fellow trustees so to act in that capacity on behalf of the charity".*

This begs the question of what is a 'profession' these days, but this clause is honoured by time and normally acceptable to the Commissioners.

That apart, the Commissioners will only accept remunerated trustees if they can be satisfied (and they take some convincing) that the particular charity has vital need of the same. Need in this context is judged in terms of the probable damage to the effectiveness of the charity of being denied one or more paid trustees. Here are some possibilities:-

(a) A charity established by the effort and the reputation of one person who will need to work full-time for it to make it a success.
(b) A large, very active charity which needs one paid, or part paid, executive trustee in order to hold its operations together and provide leadership to the board and a link with a large staff.
(c) An employee-driven community charity where keeping all staff off the governing committee will endanger its performance and even survival (e.g. most local C.A.B.s have employee representation on their committees).

The standard safeguards which the Commissioners will require are that the number of remunerated trustees always be less than a majority of the quorum and that any such trustees be absent from those parts of meetings which consider matters in which they have a personal interest.

The trustees must ensure that the charity's purposes are carried out

You can always, as a second best, consider a membership charity of which the charity employees would be permitted to be members and are thus in the position to vote. However all the implications need careful balancing.

Trustee expenses

Whether or not one seeks to have remunerated trustees, it is normal and acceptable to provide (and provision there must be) in the constitution that the trustees can be paid their out-of-pocket expenses incurred in connection with acting as trustees, as well as for payment of reasonable interest on monies lent to the trust or rent for property let to it. The standard provisos to the Memorandum of Association of a charitable company regulate this and other such matters.

Reimbursement of 'lost' earnings

Busy charities are increasingly vexed by the problem of employed trustees who will lose pay if they are assiduous in attending trustee meetings. This presupposes that many charities, because of weight of trustee business and sometimes, too, for the sake of staff involvement, need to hold some meetings during normal working hours. It is advisable to provide in the constitution for maximum daily and annual reimbursement levels, individually and for the trustees collectively. This is still a fluid area vis-a-vis the Commissioners, and will have to be negotiated on its merits case by case.

Conflict of interest

It is a principle of charity law that a trustee must seek to avoid a situation in which his or her charitable duty and his or her personal interests conflict.

This is at its most acute where, for example, a trustee is selling something to or buying something from the charity of which he or she is a trustee. This can lead to severely harsh legal consequences if special precautions are not taken to avoid the conflict by insulating the trustee from the transaction concerned. This is true, no less, of charities in corporate form, where S.320 (inter alia) of the Companies Act 1985 applies.

This handbook is not the place to fully explain this subject, and legal advice should be taken when direct or indirect conflict may be looming.

Delegation of trustees' powers

The rule is that trustees cannot delegate their powers unless the constitution of the charity expressly allows. It is important that it does. This will enable the charity, for example, to involve employees and valued outsiders on committees. If this is desired, the provision in Table C of the Companies Act 1985 will need to be extended where it is incorporated into the Articles of a corporate charity.

If a charity in trust form has the power to alter its constitution, then a delegation provision can be inserted if there is none. Corporate charities have that power under company law anyhow though advice should be taken in relation to S.64 of the Charities Act 1993.

But even where a charity has no such powers of amendment, individual trustees can take advantage of the provisions of Section 25 of the Trustee Act 1925. This allows delegation of his or her powers and discretions, in whole or part, for up to 12 months at a time so long as the delegation is done by power of Attorney.

The Charity Commission will insist that all delegated powers can be withdrawn (revoked) by the trustees at any time. It is also as well to stipulate that any committee with delegated powers must promptly inform the trustees of their decisions and activities.

Above all, it is wise to stipulate that no committee can commit the funds of the charity without express authorisation.

A busy charity may well want to operate its bank account on the signature of some, or even none, of its trustees. (See p47).

The powers of trustees

General

Trustees are bound by the more demanding as between general (non-statute) charitable law, statute law and the constitution of their particular charity.

Subject to that, the golden rule of setting up a charity is normally to give its trustees (and therefore the charity) the widest powers and discretions. For example, and always assuming that you can find trustees in whom you have confidence, you should provide complete discretion as to how the trustees can invest the charity's assets; as to whom and on what terms it can lend charity funds and borrow funds; as to how the charity is managed; as to if and when to dissolve (i.e. wind-up) the charity and then to decide as to which other charity or charitable purpose to pass any surplus.

Investment powers

In fact there is no such thing as 'complete discretion', because the general law of charity will always require honest good sense of charity trustees in all they do.

Unless the constitution otherwise expressly so allows, the trustees will be confined to investments authorised by the Trustee Investment Act 1961. Broadly speaking, this requires them to divide their funds into two halves. One can be invested in the shares of large publicly quoted U.K. companies and non U.K. companies via Unit Trusts, but the other half can only be invested in supposedly risk-free investments such as securities issued by the Government or local authorities.

However, one way of properly breaking out of the 1961 Act constraints is to invest in a Common Investment Fund (itself having unrestricted powers of investment).

But even with carte blanche trustees must generally invest as a prudent man or woman of affairs would if he or she were investing someone else's money for whom they felt morally responsible. Unless the fund is small, they should try to spread the investment to avoid having too many eggs in one basket. They should also normally have the advice of a trustee with experience in the investment world or take professional advice.

Trustees must generally strike a balance between a good return, decent capital growth and security. They should never gamble. (For fuller details see 'Charity Investment' - Further Reading).

Ethical investment

The question many charity trustees are asking themselves is whether or not, by law, they must give paramount consideration to purely financial considerations when investing, or whether they can or must subjugate that to non-financial factors. The view until relatively recently was that one can only take account of what are called ethical considerations if there is no financial 'cost', in terms of income, capital growth or security. This has had much to do with a narrow reading of the judgement in Cowan -v- Scargill (which was not in any event a charity case).

In their report for 1987 the Charity Commissioners for the first time gave advice on ethical investment policy. The nub of it was that:

> *'whilst the normal duty of charity trustees in exercising their investment powers is to provide the greatest financial benefits, financial return is not in all cases the sole consideration. Charity trustees should not invest in companies pursuing activities which are directly contrary to the purposes or trusts of their charity. It would, for example, be entirely appropriate for the trustees of cancer relief charities to decline to invest in tobacco companies'.*

This is really a simple point. Anything and everything which trustees decide for and on behalf of their charity must be consistent with its charitable purposes. Where they are broad and general, the ethical considerations are likely to be less intrusive. Where, however, the purposes are particular, then certain investments will not only be ill-advised, they may even be unlawful, whatever the financial benefits accruing. These dilemmas are likely to be more acute for religious charities.

Furthermore, the trustees should take account of the impact of sensitive investments on its donors, on would-be donors and on its standing with its beneficiaries.

These issues were canvassed in the recent case of the Bishop of Oxford -v- Church Commissioners.

The difficulty, of course, is in forming a sensible judgement as to the extent to which it is proper to take account of such non-financial criteria. Circumstances will change. The danger is that some trustees may allow personal prejudice to get in the way of a genuine attempt at objective evaluation.

However, in the changing world investment climate, it is likely that more and more charities will be exercised by the task of trying to invest in a manner ethically compatible with their objects.

Appointment and replacement of trustees

The usual system is that trustees of a charitable trust hold office until and unless they retire or are removed. In a trust set up by an individual it is not unusual to provide that the power of appointment is exercisable by the founder. Where nothing is provided, the Trustee Act gives power of appointment to the continuing trustees. In the case of corporate charities Table C of the Companies Act is often followed, which provides for automatic retirement by rotation of trustee-directors after three years in office.

In any event your constitution should specify who has the power to appoint and remove trustees. If it is a corporate charity these powers invariably reside in the members, who can number donors, employees and even (potential) beneficiaries in their ranks. However, other arrangements can be set up. For example, Citizens Advice Bureaux elect their local committees at open meetings to which any local person can attend and vote. (Note, however, that if the charity is a company nothing can deprive its *members* of the right to remove any or all of its trustees/directors at any time).

The Charity Commissioners have extensive power to discharge trustees and officers of a charity in cases of misconduct or mismanagement. They may also remove a charity trustee where he or she has been convicted of a serious crime, is bankrupt, is incapable of acting by reason of mental disorder or when a trustee's failure to act impedes the proper administration of the charity. Any person interested in a charity's affairs can make representation to the Charity Commission to that end.

The Charities Act 1992 for the first time introduced prohibitions on certain categories of person being appointed, or continuing, as charity trustees, and the Charity Commission now has to keep a register of such incapables. There are criminal sanctions for breach of the prohibitions.

Charity accounts

Whether or not you have your accounts audited (see Tables 2 and 3) it is most important to institute an appropriate book-keeping system from day one. Small charities can use very simple systems but if you fail to set one up early enough or fail to operate it assiduously you will store up time-consuming problems for yourselves and will not be able to keep financial control and effective management. Furthermore, without evidence of proper financial systems you may find it difficult to obtain funding.

Charity stationery

If the charity is a company or IPS then the word 'limited' must appear as the last word of the name unless a special statutory declaration is filed at Companies House or unless you obtain permission from the Registry of Friendly Societies. In either case your stationery must still state that the charity is a limited company or IPS.

The stationery of companies should also state the place of registration of the company, its registered company number and the address of its registered office. If you name any directors, you must name them all.

Since the Charities Act 1992 it is now essential for registered charities to state the fact that they are so registered.

7.

The Charities Acts 1992 and 1993

Registration, administration, accounting and reporting etc.

Generally, as already noted, there is still more subsidiary legislation to come under the provisions of the 1992 and 1993 Charities Acts particularly concerning the fees the Commission will be charging, the detailed accounting provisions, detailed regulations concerning professional fundraising and public charitable collections. The timetable for this has been put back so that the recommendations of the Deregulation Task Force for the charity sector, established in late summer 1993, can be considered and implemented.

On top of all this, the demanding Statement of Recommended Practice (SORP 2) for charity accounts is nearing finalisation.

It is beyond the scope of this handbook to detail all this. The Charity Commission will be issuing guidance publications, and one book - 'Charities - The New Law' (see Reading List) - has already covered the new legislation in some detail.

Some key contents of the 1993 Act:

- charity registration requirements (see s.3 and Table 1 of this handbook); power to force a change in a charity's name (s.6) and (importantly) the requirement for the fact of registration to appear on a charity's notepaper etc. (s.5 and see Table 1);
- the 1993 Act extends the already wide powers of the Commissioners to inquire into, and protect, the affairs of charities (ss.8-12, 16-20) including power to bring proceedings (ss.32-34, 87-90);
- arrangements for the Commissioners to make

Charitable Status

Table 1. The need to register under the Charities Acts

This table indicates, according to charity type, the need for a charity to register under s3 of the 1993 Act, to declare its status as a registered charity under s5 of the 1993 Act, if its income in the last financial year exceeded £5,000 and to declare its status as a charity under s68 of the 1993 Act, if the name 'charity' or 'charitable' does not appear in the name of the charity.

Key to charity types

1. *Exempt charity, including industrial and provident society.*
2. *Charity excepted from registration by order or regulation.*
3. *Charity with permanent endowment, not falling into categories 1 or 2.*
4. *Charity having use or occupation of land, not falling into categories 1 or 2*
5. *Charity with gross income in excess of £10,000 a year, not falling into categories 1 or 2.*
6. *Charity with gross income not exceeding £10,000 a year, or falling into categories 1 or 4.*

Charity type	Registration	Declaration of registered status*	Declaration of charitable status**
1	None possible	Not applicable	If a company
2	Voluntary	Compulsory	If a company
3	Compulsory	Compulsory	If a company
4	Compulsory	Compulsory	If a company
5	Compulsory	Compulsory	If a company
6	Voluntary	Not compulsory	If a company

* *If income in the last financial year exceeded £5,000*
** *If the word 'charity' or 'charitable' does not appear in the name.*

"Schemes" extending charities' objects (ss.13-15);
- more liberal, self-policing arrangements for selling, leasing and mortgaging charity property etc. (ss.36-40);
- a new regime for accounts, reports and returns, including audits and rights of public inspection (ss.41-49 and see Tables 2 and 3 of this handbook);
- arrangements re incorporation of charity trustees and charitable companies (ss.50-69);
- extended disqualification arrangements for, and a register of, charity trustees (ss.72-73);
- other provisions concerning investment, advice to charity trustees, control of solicitors costs, ex gratia payments by charities, small and local charities, notice for charity meetings, appeals from Charity Commission decisions, registry of charity documents.

Some key contents of the 1992 Act :

- control on professional fundraising (see p66) (Part II of the 1992 Act);
- control of Public Collections (see p69) (Part III of the 1992 Act)

Annual accounts, audits, reports and returns etc. after the 1992 and 1993 Acts

Tables 1, 2 and 3 of this handbook summarise what each type of charity must do every year in relation to accounts, audits, reports and returns. The following should also be noted:-

(a) The Act distinguishes between basic 'accounting records' (accurate entries and records from which accounts can be prepared - s.41); simplified 'receipts and payments account and a statement of assets and liabilities' (simplified accounts - s.42(3)); accruals 'statement of accounts complying with such requirements as to its form and contents as may be prescribed by regulations' (full accounts for which subsidiary legislation is awaited - s.42(1)).

(b) Charitable companies are affected by some of the new requirements, but not all, but in any event remain subject to company and charity law. (See the Tables.)

Table 2. Registered Charities

This table shows the accounting and reporting requirements of registered charities according to the charity type. A charity may also be subject to other accounting and reporting regimes not shown in the table. Except where otherwise stated, section numbers refer to the Charities Act 1993.

Key to registered charities.

1. *With gross income or total expenditure exceeding £100,000.*
2. *With gross income between £25,000 and £100,000.*
3. *With gross income between £10,000 and £25,000.*
4. *With annual income below £10,000 (voluntary registration).*
5. *Charitable company regardless of income.*
6. *Excepted charity, registered on voluntary basis.*

Charity type	Accounting records (s41)	Annual accounts (s42)	Audit independent examination (s43)	Annual report (s45)	Annual Return (s48)	Accounts to public (s47)
1	Yes	Full accounts	Full audit	Yes	Yes	Yes
2	Yes	Full accounts	Independent Examination	Yes	Yes	Yes
3	Yes	Simplified accounts	Independent Examination	Yes	Yes	Yes
4	Yes	Simplified accounts	Independent Examination	Yes	Yes	Yes
5	No but must comply with Companies Act 1985	No but must comply with Companies Act 1985	No but subject to s69 and must comply with Companies Act 1989	Yes in addition to Companies Act 1985	Yes in addition to Companies Act 1985	Yes
6.	Yes	Full accounts if income over £25,000: simplified accounts if below	Full audit if gross income over £100,000, otherwise independent examination	Yes	Yes	Yes

(c) A full audit is not required for a charity whose gross annual income or total expenditure is £100,000 or under. In that event, if it is not a corporate charity, an 'independent examination' will be sufficient, that is to say an examination by an independent person who is reasonably believed by the trustees to have the requisite ability and practical experience to carry out a competent examination of the accounts (s.43(3)). The Charity Commission can give clearance if a charity wants to check if someone is within this definition, and may publish directions.

(d) Every registered charity, in whatever form, must make an annual report within 10 months of its year end on its activities containing such information as prescribed by subsidiary legislation (s.45). These reports will be open to public inspection.

(e) In addition, such charities must also submit to the Commissioners an annual return (s.48), the difference being that its scope is determined by the Commissioners, and it is not on public view.

[Note: At the time of going to press it is clear that the above regulatory framework in the light of the Deregulation Task Force recommendations will be significantly liberalised, probably before the end of 1994.]

Offences under the 1993 Act

Contrary to the advice of Sir Philip Woodfield in his report and Home Secretary Hurd in his White Paper there are criminal sanctions (prosecution in the magistrates courts) for trustees who 'without reasonable excuse' are 'persistently in default' of these reporting and accounting requirements. It is the same for failings in relation to the publicity requirements of s.5. Consent of the Director of Public Prosecutions is required to any prosecution, and the Government spokesman in debate assured peers that prosecution would only take place in 'most extreme cases'.

Exempt charities

Some charities have been accorded the privilege of being exempt from many of the administrative provisions of the Charities Act 1993. They do not have to - indeed cannot

Table 3. Unregistered Charities

This table shows the accounting and reporting requirements of unregistered charities according to the charity type. A charity may also be subject to other statutory regimes not shown in the table. Except otherwise stated, section numbers refer to the Charities Act 1993.

Key to registered charities.

1. *Exempt Charity.*
2. *Unregistered charitable company, regardless of income.*
3. *Charity (other than company) with annual income below £10,000.*
4. *Excepted charity with annual income exceeding £10,000, but not registered on voluntary basis.*

Charity type	Accounting records (s41)	Annual accounts (s42)	Audit independent examination (s43)	Annual report (s45)	Annual Return (s48)	Accounts to public (s47)
1	No but must comply with s46	No but must comply with s46	None	None	None	Yes
2	No but must comply with Companies Act 1985	No but must comply with Companies Act 1985	No but subject to s69 and must comply with Companies Act 1989	No but must comply with Companies Act 1985	No but must comply with Companies Act 1985	Yes
3	Yes	Simplified Accounts	None	None	None	Yes
4	Yes	Full accounts if gross income over £25,000; simplified accounts if below £25,000	Full audit if gross income over £100,000; otherwise independent examination	On request	None	Yes

- register with the Charity Commission (s.3), nor have to produce full accounts or annual reports or returns to the Charity Commission. For fuller details see Tables 1 and 3.

They are also free of the land dealing requirements (s.36) though they are subject to the fundraising and public collection regimes under the 1993 Act.

Some main categories of exempt charities are those which are Industrial and Provident Society or Friendly Societies; grant-maintained schools; universities; major museums etc.; most mainstream churches and chapels. For the full list see Schedule 2 to the 1993 Act.

Excepted charities

There is a separate category of charities which, though not exempt, are excepted by order or regulation from the need to register. They are also treated differently in some other respects concerning accounts, reports etc. (see Tables 1, 2 and 3).

Small charities

Those charities neither having any permanent endowment, nor annual income of over £1,000, nor the use or occupation of any land, can choose whether or not to register; need not publicise their registered status and (if not registered) are free from annual accounts (though they must keep S41 records) audits, reports and returns.

Fundraising

Fundraising for most local charities is normally a matter of chance and circumstance. Raffles, bazaars, 'events' and high street collections have been standbys, but things are changing. The larger charity, with paid staff, long-term projects and some contract funding will almost certainly be caught up in more sophisticated ways of raising money, sometimes involving the services of professional fundraisers or alternatively 'deals' with a commercial sponsor. Deals they are, because the *commercial participator* (as the Charities Act 1992 calls the organisation working with the charity) is certainly not giving something for nothing. The charity will be providing the commercial participator with, for example, access to its mailing list or some form of passive endorsement.

Part II of the 1992 Act, which comes into force in late 1994, sets out a completely new and complicated regulatory framework to control fundraising. It is not intended to affect fundraising either by a charity's trading company or by the charity all on its own.

Professional Fundraisers

An individual or business engaged in the business of raising funds for a specific charity or charities for reward is likely to be a professional fundraiser under the 1992 Act. Merely giving advice on how to raise funds will not be caught.

Examples of professional fundraising are direct mail companies which write in their own name to potential donors and telephone fundraisers who likewise telephonically solicit donations of pledges. (Note that as regards the latter, including broadcast appeals where payment is by debit or credit card, Sections 60/61 of the 1992 Act give the donor the right to revoke any donation in excess of £50 so long as done within seven days of either receiving a written statement from the telephone fundraiser - as is required - or of the broadcast appeal. Such a written statement is in addition to the general need for the 'statement' described below.)

Note that small-scale fundraising (defined in s.58(3) of the 1992 Act) is not within the definition of 'professional fundraising'.

Requirements made of a professional fundraiser

You must have an agreement with the professional fundraiser which satisfies the requirements of Section 59(1) of the 1992 Act. The draft regulations (yet to be published) state that the agreement must be in writing, include the name and address of each party, the date, the period of the agreement, arrangements for earlier termination and for variation. It must also contain a statement of the principal objectives and methods to be used, and (vitally) details of the entitlement of the fundraiser to remuneration and expenses.

The professional fundraiser must accompany each 'solicitation' (very widely defined) with a statement clearly indicating the name of the beneficiary charity or charities (and which gets what) and how the fundraiser's remuneration is to be determined (for example, a fixed fee or percentage). (Note - this last part of the legislation is faultily drafted, and will no doubt be amended in due course - s.60(3)).

A professional fundraiser?

Commercial Participators

If a charity agrees with a business to aid or support, directly or indirectly, the public to purchase its goods or services in return for some payment or other benefit (sometimes called sponsorship), then it is likely that the business will be a "commercial participator".

Examples are where a charity enters into an agreement with a drink retailer or manufacturer where 1p per bottle sold bearing the charity's logo will go to it, or where a bank pays to a charity a small percentage of the value of purchases transacted with the bank's credit cards bearing the charity's logo and/or name.

Requirements made of a Commercial Participator

There must be an agreement with the commercial participator under Section 59(2) similar to that outlined for professional fund-raisers.

A commercial participator must also accompany each representation it makes with a statement clearly indicating the name of your charity (and the other institutions involved) and the proportion(s) in which you (and the other institutions) are to benefit and the method which is to be used to calculate what moneys from the proceeds of sale of the goods or services are to go to your charity.

Use of an affinity credit card is likely to be such a 'representation' requiring the statutory statement (see s.60 and s.58(6)).

Effects of failure to comply with the 1992 Act

After they come into effect any agreement which does not comply with the Regulations will be unenforceable without the sanction of the court. Furthermore, a failure to make the required statements by the professional fundraiser and/or commercial participator will be an offence punishable on summary conviction by a fine not exceeding £5,000.

Notes about sponsorship deals etc

a) The above is only a summary of the Act. If you think what you plan to do is at all borderline make sure to check with an expert before you risk operating without meeting the Act's requirements.

b) A charity is not empowered by its objects to carry on permanent or substantial trade which is not a direct carrying out of those objects or ancillary to them (and structured trading activities to raise funds is not such).

c) Deals with commercial sponsors to allow them to use, or exploit, the charity's name, goodwill, logo or to access the charity's membership or supporters, is likely to be trade, if the charity is an active partner.

d) That is likely to give rise to tax and VAT issues. Often it is best to structure the arrangements via a trading company owned by the charity, because it can covenant its profits in tax-free form back to the charity. However, where possible, the charity should take its reward direct as a 'royalty' (which is tax exempt in the charity's hands, unlike other trading profits it makes - see section below).

e) However, the charity must never enter into a fundraising arrangement which is inconsistent with, or likely to significantly damage, its reputation or its work. Thus, if it structures part of the 'deal' via its trading company, it must ensure that the trading company likewise protects the charity, especially if its name incorporates the charity's name.

f) Lastly, you should seek expert advice on possible mitigation of VAT which generally bites on the charity no differently from its trading company. Often the Inland Revenue and Customs and Excise will accept a split in receipts from a sponsor between taxable, VATable payments and donations direct to the charity.

Public Charitable Collections

Part III of the 1992 Act (which is likely to be amended before it comes into effect) will regulate Public Charitable Collections conducted by a charity or by someone on its behalf. The existing legislation only regulates street or house-to-house collections, but the new Act has far stickier regulatory tentacles and will cover such impromptu frolics as Christmas carol singing!

Your charity will then have to obtain a Local Authority permit under Section 68 or (if the charity is collecting throughout a substantial part of England and Wales) an order from the Charity Commission under Section 72 if you plan any of the following:-

1. a) Collecting in person money or other property (e.g. jumble, stamps, books, newspapers and food) whether or not you are offering anything in return (Section 65(a)(b)); or

   b) Offering goods or services for sale e.g. a house to house sale of goods which (for example) have been made by people with learning disabilities (Section 65(7)); and

2. Representing that the whole or part of the proceeds will go to charity or for some other benevolent or philanthropic purpose (Section 65(a)(b); and

Charitable Status

3. The collection is taking place in the street or by visits from house to house or an outdoor public place to which the public are admitted or have access including a station, airport, shopping precinct or similar public area e.g. car park (Section 65(8)(b)). The latter does not include access given purely for the purposes of fundraising (e.g. a whist drive) nor where a payment or a ticket is required (e.g. a summer fete (Section 65(9))).

Obtaining permits

It is the duty of the person who organises or controls the conduct of the collection to apply for the permit (Section 65(3)). Detailed regulations have yet to be issued. The Act contains an appeal procedure both against any conditions attached to a permit as well as against a refusal to issue a permit. It is a criminal offence to apply for a permit falsely or carelessly. Again, regulations are to be made to amplify all these procedures.

8.

Liability of trustees/ directors

In this chapter charity trustees will be taken (unless otherwise indicated) to refer to the trustees of a charitable trust, the directors (however called e.g. members of the Council of Management) of a charitable company and the committee members (however called) of an unincorporated society, association or club which is also a charity.

Personal liability
(see Liability of trustees/directors pages 38/39)

Where a charity trustee acts dishonestly (deceitfully), or recklessly or with wilful negligence, or allows his or her charity to act outside the scope of its constitution (or as lawyers say ultra vires), he or she is likely to be personally liable without limit to whoever incurs loss as a result and/or to the charity itself. Unless the trustee or trustees concerned get relief from such liability from the High Court or the Charity Commission, which they have little hope of doing in such cases, they will have to find money out of their own pockets, and cannot reimburse themselves out of the assets of the charity, however considerable they may be. Furthermore, in none of these cases will the trustees be covered by any indemnity insurance.

Possible personal liability

Where loss is incurred by a charity through inadvertent breach of trust or other negligence by its trustees, short of the culpability inherent in the cases just referred to, they can be called to personal account by the court or the Charity Commission and made personally liable. However, that will be a rarity, and both the court and Commission have a discretion to relieve trustees of personal liability in such cases and usually

Charitable Status

Trustee liability is a personal one

will. However, where such breach or negligence causes a third party loss or damage which is uninsured and which the charity, being unincorporated, does not have the assets to meet, the trustees will remain personally liable, and cannot be relieved.

Limited liability

Apart from the circumstance just mentioned, where the trustee of an incorporated charity is at some advantage (though it is usually exaggerated), liability may seem to arise where the charity becomes insolvent because of unforeseen events or in circumstances where its trustees/directors cannot be said to be responsible. This could be where its debts had piled up in circumstances where there was no "wrongful trading" (see p39), or where some sudden and unpredictable cancellation of funding occurred. Trustees will not be personally liable for the unmet debts of the charity.

Unincorporated charities

Although trustees will normally be entitled to subsequent reimbursement of moneys spent meeting the charity's liabilities to third parties if their charity obtains or raises further funds, that may well not be the case if the liability arose because of some fault or negligence on their part (even though inadvertent). This is where indemnity insurance can provide solace.

With regard to unincorporated membership associations, it is worth noting that the committee can only reimburse itself by levying the membership if the constitution clearly gives them that power or if the members had sanctioned the particular liability.

Further, although an action against an unincorporated charity will have to be commenced against those who are currently its governing body, actual liability will attach to those who were on that body at the time the liability was incurred.

Liability of trustees/ directors

If charity trustees are worried about whether a proposed course of action on behalf of the charity is proper, they had better seek advice from a solicitor or the Charity Commission, though the advice of the latter is likely to be conservative and can be a long time a-coming.

However, advice given by the Commission in knowledge of the full facts serves as some real protection for the charity trustees who act on it, because their action cannot then be regarded as a breach of trust (see section 29 of the Charities Act 1993).

Trustees indemnity insurance

If the constitution of the charity so allows, or if the Charity Commission agree to an alteration so to allow (which will not be possible without a scheme unless its constitution contains a power to amend) it is now possible for a charity to take out and pay for an indemnity policy to cover its trustees' risks of personal liability. Such cover will not cover the personal liability of a trustee caused by his/her recklessness, wilful negligence or dishonesty. It should also be remembered that insurance will not protect trustees of unincorporated charities from straightforward contractual liabilities the charity has not the assets to meet.

9.

Charities, politics and campaigning

Charities are not permitted to have directly political objects. They are therefore restricted in the nature and extent of the campaigning work they can undertake. Amnesty International fell foul of this rule. But charities can also be over-cautious.

The law allows a degree of political activity by charities if it is in pursuit of their objects. As the Charity Commissioners put it in their report for 1976, "... a charity is not prohibited from engaging in political activities provided that these are carried out in furtherance of its objects". The White Paper on Charities of 1989 was similarly liberal.

What is clear is that a body which has as an object to change the law in some way cannot be registered as a charity. Further, regardless of its objects, if the main weight of a charity's activity is directed to changing the law it will be acting outside charitable limits.

Permissible political activity

Thus, provided that the political activity is directly ancillary to or otherwise in furtherance of its charitable objects, a charity is allowed to:-

(a) provide information and advice when this is requested by government officials; presenting reasoned memoranda to MPs and ministers
(b) comment on Green or White Papers
(c) provide members of either House of Parliament with non-partisan advice and information especially from their on-ground experience, for or against a published Bill and any amendments, and even to draft amendments relevant to their objects.

(d) in some other cases, not involving legislation, a charity is entitled to lobby Members to support its cause in Parliament. For instance, where the question arises whether a government grant is to be made or continued to a particular charity or country whose poor it seeks to help.

(e) carry on some non party-political parliamentary activity, as for example supporting enabling legislation granting a charity wider powers to carry out its purposes.

(f) educate the public in a rational way concerning the needs it meets and ways of ameliorating them, particularly by telling people of the direct experiences of its beneficiaries.

If the political activities you envisage fall outside these categories, they may still be permissible if they are directly ancillary to the main objects of your charity and do not absorb too substantial or regular a part of your charity's resources. For example, it may well be lawful for an information campaign to be organised by a disaster relief charity, the means of which must be appropriate to the circumstances, to persuade the government to intervene with taxpayers' money in some overseas tragedy.

Similarly, for a housing charity to canvas for greater allocation of national resources for the homeless would not itself put that organisation beyond the charitable pale.

At the time of going to press the Charity Commission were about to introduce a revised (and improved) version of their free booklet, Political Activities by Charities, which was based upon the advice contained in their 1981 annual report. (See Further Reading.)

It is fair to point out, though, that this is sensitive territory for the Charity Commission. Above all, in any political activity a charity should be non-partisan, objective, balanced, even-handed and strike the appropriate tone.

Sanctions for excess

If, for example, a charity is found to have engaged in impermissible political activities the trustees may in extremis be asked to pay to the charity the funds which have been misapplied. The charity may also have to forfeit to the Inland Revenue the tax relief on the misapplied funds, but will not lose its charitable status. That would be to punish the public (for

Charities are not permitted to have directly political objects

a charity is such) for the failings of its trustees. (See Loss of Tax Exemptions, p90).

It is unfortunate that the House of Lords, the highest court in the land, has not lately had the opportunity of clarifying the limits of political activity. The extension of statute and EC law into every corner of our day-to-day lives makes it impossible for the socially concerned charity to operate 'beyond' politics.

Parallel political organisations

Several charities, realising that some of their proposed activities would fall the wrong side of the shadowy dividing line between what is and what is not permitted by way of political activity, have established separate non-charitable organisations to carry on those functions. On other occasions a non-charitable organisation has hived off its charitable activities. The National Council for Civil Liberties, Public Interest Research Centre and Amnesty International are all examples of this. It is incumbent upon the charity to avoid confusion between the two bodies in such cases.

The Charity Commissioners are sometimes uneasy that this separation of the two parallel organisations may in practice degenerate into a single muddle. In practice it is essential to prepare the ground thoroughly so that the mechanics of cost apportionment and cross-accounting between two bodies have been properly resolved and are duly implemented.

General conclusions

In practice the Charity Commission is patient with established charities over any quasi-political activities which they undertake. This sensitive area of charity practice is one in which a good deal of tact and restraint has avoided, thus far, too many collisions.

Education and propaganda

The distinction between public education, which is permitted to charities, and propaganda, which isn't, is sometimes a fine one. A vigorous campaign run by a charity to inform the public of the needs of its beneficiaries should be acceptable so long as people are objectively informed, unless the charity is merely advancing an ideological solution to a problem. This then strays into propaganda, lacking the necessary rationality and balance.

Think tanks

In recent years a number of charitable research organisations have been very active, such as the (rightish) Adam Smith Institute and Institute of Economic Affairs and now the (leftish) Institute for Public Policy Research. In the light of the sensitivity occasionally manifested on Parliament's back benches against 'politicking' by charities, it is a source of wonderment that charities such as these have not been tarred and feathered. They manage to stay inside the ropes by packing their committees with the great and good and having the sense to maintain some semblance of political balance amongst them.

Tailpiece

For charities which find themselves butting against these hazy frontiers in seeking to do the best by their charitable purposes it is highly advisable that they develop for their staff and supporters a protocol of 'do's and don'ts'. This can prevent misunderstanding, or worse.

10.

Charities and money earning

Can charities trade?

Trade as such is not a charitable object even though it provides the funds for a charity to do its work. But it is prudent to give a charity the power to trade from the outset. So long as the trade is modest in amount (occasional fundraising activities) there is little danger of the balance of activities getting out of gear through the trade ceasing to be merely ancillary and becoming a mainstream activity.

In two cases, however, trade may be allowable by charity law, and exempt under tax law. The first is where the trade is a direct and actual implementation of the very objects of the charity. For example, the provision of educational services by an educational charity.

The second is where the trade is mainly carried out by the beneficiaries of the charity, as well as implementing its objects. Only in a few rare instances does this happy coincidence occur, for example workshops for the blind which produce goods for sale in the course of the rehabilitation of those for whom the charity exists.

Charities increasingly rely on self-help to keep themselves going. The begging bowl appears to be giving way to contract and trading activities of one kind or another, such as mail-order selling, charity shops, retailing third world products and the sale of Christmas cards. Affinity credit cards are another recent development.

The contract culture - charging for services

One of the key questions in budgeting for a charity is whether or not it can charge for services rendered by it. Here we are not considering services in the nature of trade, but benefits which a charity bestows on people in the course of furthering its charitable purposes. This is a massively burgeoning aspect of charity life and times today.

One only has to realise that most 'independent' schools and 'private' hospitals are registered charities to realise not only that a charity may charge but that it can charge heavily.

Charities and money earning

Many charities today survive by purveying services to individuals (e.g. the elderly), to government (e.g. training schemes or mental health care) and even to business (e.g. research). There is usually no tax or vires problem, though trustees do need to beware against over-commitment to a single 'client' and, as part of that, to taking on long-term expenses which are only covered by short-term funding. Reform of contracting arrangements with government, in particular, is long overdue.

One must also introduce a word of warning against making charges so high that the charity could endanger its status by ceasing to benefit the public.

Frequently, however, a charity will find that even though there is an apparent profit on a charge, if it adds the real costs of providing the service there is no true, or net, profit.

Even then, a charity may be perfectly justified in structuring a 'trading' surplus to provide for necessary capital investment and future development for the benefit of the charity.

Benefits to the donor

A gift is not a gift for tax purposes if the donor receives a benefit in return. Where Gift Aid is concerned the legislation specifies that any benefit to the donor equivalent to more than 2½% of the value of the gift, subject to an overall ceiling of £250 will negate the whole of it for tax purposes.

There is no such hard and fast rule for covenants, but there are clear conventions (for example the Inland Revenue will not cancel the tax benefits if members only receive a newsletter or magazine) and these need checking in each case.

The National Trust, for example, are allowed to collect membership subscriptions by covenant despite those covenanting enjoying free admission to Trust properties, plus receipt of a regular magazine.

Occasional fundraising

Fundraising which involves charging people, and which is carried out on a regular basis, stands the risk of being treated as a taxable 'trade' by the Inland Revenue and taxed accordingly, at corporation tax rates. However, by concession the Inland Revenue will not seek to tax the funds raised so long as the following conditions are satisfied:

(1) The organisation is not regularly trading;
(2) The trading is not in competition with other traders;
(3) The activities are supported substantially because the public are aware that any profits will be devoted to charity;
(4) The profits are transferred to charities or otherwise applied for charitable purposes.

See Inland Revenue leaflet C5.

How to trade safely - the trading company

The common method used to engage in substantial trade (which is not in fulfilment of the charity's primary purpose) is for a separate trading organisation, usually a company with share capital and limited liability, to be established for or by the charity. This company is not subject to the laws of charity, and so is free to trade more or less like any commercial company. So long as the trading company covenants (i.e. commits by deed) to pay its profits (both revenue and capital) for a period exceeding three years to the charity, or donates its profits under the Gift Aid scheme, the net result is broadly the same in terms of tax as if the charity had been allowed to carry out the trade tax free itself. In short, no corporation tax will be paid and all the profits can be passed to the charity.

The begging bowl - giving way to trading

Tax formalities, trading risks

If the trading company retains some of the profit, it will (subject to the availability of other set-offs and reliefs) be subject to corporation tax. It may well be necessary to take professional advice on this.

The trading company must retain tax at basic income tax rate out of its covenanted or Gift Aid payment, and account for the same to the Inland Revenue. The Inland Revenue has agreed that claims by charities to recover that tax will normally be speeded up. The detailed arrangements are contained at the back of the free Inland Revenue booklet Tax Relief for Charities (ref. IR75) (see Further Reading). The speedy procedure is not available for all tax repayments.

Trading through a separate limited company in this way has the advantage that it will insulate the funds of the charity against the risks of something going wrong with the trade, when the liability of the trading company will be limited by law to the extent of its own assets. A charity should, however, beware of putting this insulation at risk by using a similar name and logo for its trading company and encouraging members of the public to think that they are trading with the charity itself.

Can the charity finance its trading company?

Strictly speaking the charity can only use its funds to pursue its objects or, meanwhile, to invest as its constitution allows. If a charity wants to establish a wholly-owned trading company, on the above lines, the charity should make sure from the outset that its constitution permits the trustees to invest in the shares of a private company.

Similarly, if the trading company is going to need loan facilities, the investment powers of the charity should make it clear from the outset that the trustees are free to make loans without security to any company in which the charity holds shares. Such a loan must also be prudent.

Since the Finance Act 1986 trustees will need to get the clearance of the Inland Revenue where they want to make loans if there is any danger that they will otherwise start to lose some of their tax exemptions according to the rather complex tests (see Loss of Tax Exemptions). To get consent the Inland Revenue must be satisfied that the loan is to be made 'for the benefit of the charity and not for the avoidance of tax (whether by the charity or any other person)'. Loans to subsidiaries are not considered to be of that kind.

As to prudence, in making loans, regard must be had to the need for repayment. As already mentioned, it is not within the power of trustees simply to avoid the embarrassment of a trading company going into insolvency by making regular loans to it. However, the terms for loans can be realistic in all the circumstances. That is to say, as long as the package of conditions looks commercially reasonable from the standpoint of a lender and a borrower in such close relationship (bearing in mind that the trading company will hopefully not only repay the loan some time, but yield much greater benefits to the charity in the form of covenanted profits) all should be well.

Finally, it has to be remembered that repayment of the loan can only come out of the trading company's profits after tax, and if it has covenanted all its profits back to the charity there will be nothing left with which to make repayments. Expert advice on all this must be taken if the loans represent a significant part of the charity's assets, or a significant chunk of the trading company's working capital.

Because of these complications, and the overheads of running a trading company separate from the charity, it will usually be best to put what trade the charity can properly undertake itself through the charity.

Separating the charity and the trading company

If a charity sets up a separate trading company on the above lines mentioned above, it is vital that the activities of the two are kept separate. What is more, since the charity generally cannot trade as a principal objective, it will be in breach of its constitution for its funds to be used simply to subsidise the trading company.

It is also vital to realise that the charity and trading company are not only different legal entities, but of a different legal nature. They must, therefore, deal with each other at arm's length, although some commercial recognition of the particularity of their relationship is warrantable. What is not, for example, is for the charity to speculate via its trading company in a way it could not itself. For example, it would not be lawful for a charity to make loans to its trading company for the latter merely to invest in highly speculative money market instruments which were outside the charity's own investment powers.

As to administration, insofar as the two organisations share premises and facilities and insofar as personnel of the charity may from time to time spend some of their working hours on the business of the trading company, the expenses, rents and wages involved should be fairly divided between the charity and the trading company. In this way no hidden subsidy of the trading company takes place at the expense of the charity.

One simple way of doing this is to keep time records if one of the charity's employees spends normal working hours on trading company business. The rate to be charged should, of course, take account of overheads. Shared premises can be dealt with on a square footage basis, not forgetting once again to charge the trading company a fair proportion of the cost of common parts (corridors, toilets etc.) and other overheads such as insurance.

11.

Charities and tax relief

There have been major changes in tax laws vis-a-vis charities in recent years. Exemptions are now more generous, but anti-abuse measures are more fierce (and not before time).

Taxes payable by charities and their donors

Income tax and corporation tax

Under Section 505 of the Income and Corporation Taxes Act 1988 all the income of charities is normally exempt from income tax and corporation tax so long as it is applied (see below) for charitable purposes. (See chapter concerning profits and trading by charities). Exemptions under Section 505 are administered by the Inland Revenue. In the case of charities which are registered with the Charity Commission, relief will invariably be granted. Even if not registered, the S.505 reliefs will be available to those which can show that they are 'established' here as charities.

'Applied' does not mean that the charity must use or spend the income in the same year as it is received. It can be intentionally accumulated. (See the section on Loss of Tax Exemptions, p90).

Stamp Duty

Charities are exempt.

'Four Year' Covenants - Income Tax benefits

The Charity: Where an individual promises (i.e. covenants) to give to charity a sum of money out of his or her taxable income for more than three consecutive years (subject to intervening death) and that promise is made by Deed (that is to say formally executed as a deed) then the charity which would benefit from this promise is by law entitled to recover from the Inland Revenue income tax at basic rate on the amount of the annual donation. The effect is to divert that tax from the state to the charity so that the donor can properly consider that the true amount of the gift includes the basic rate tax which the charity will recover.

The Giver: Before the 1980 budget a giver paying tax at higher rates (i.e. above basic rate) had to pay covenanted gifts out of his or her income after the full tax bite, though the charity could only recover basic rate tax.

Charities and tax relief

Since then the covenantor has been allowed to set off the gift against his or her higher rate tax liability.

Thus, if I normally pay tax at 40% and covenant £100 gross a year to charity, I will account to the Inland Revenue for the £25 and pay the charity £75; it will recover £25 (basic rate income tax) and I will not pay the extra £15 tax. That, too, encourages giving by covenant.

'Four Year' Covenant - Corporation Tax benefits

Where a limited company makes a covenant similar to that of the individual (i.e. for over three years and by Deed) it can make those payments out of its profits before corporation tax. That is to say the donations will be a charge on its income and so deductible in computing its liability to corporation tax. Since that tax is now running at 33% for companies with profits over £250,000 and 25% under that level, the encouragement to corporate giving is still significant.

NB1 As a matter of mechanics the company is required to deduct tax at basic rate and hand it over to the Inland Revenue from whom the charity must recover it. To minimise delay in obtaining repayment the Inland Revenue will in appropriate cases make a provisional repayment pending completion of their verification (see Inland Revenue Statement of Practice 3/87 dated 26th March 1987).

NB2 The relevant law is now consolidated in the Income & Corporation Taxes Act 1988.

Variable Covenant

Whether the four-year covenant is made by an individual or a company, it is essential that the formula in the covenant for calculating the amount to be paid to the charity year by year is precise - i.e. can only yield one (albeit variable) result. Usually the covenant is for a fixed amount. But it is in order, for example, so as to avoid a company having to make big payments in a year when its profits are low, to covenant a percentage of its profits, perhaps with a profit floor below which the percentage does not bite. The percentage formula can be as sophisticated as the company likes.

An individual trading alone or in partnership (partners are taxed individually) can make a similar covenant.


```
Gift by Deed of Covenant
Dated

I ........................................
of .......................................
..........................................
HEREBY COVENANT with (registered name of
charity) ............................ (the
'Charity') that for a period of four years
from the ...... day of .............. 19
............. or during my life (whichever
period be the shorter) I will pay annually/
quarterly/monthly to the Charity out of my
taxable income £ .........................
(sum in words) ...........................
Signed and delivered as his deed by the
covenantor ...............................

In the presence of .......................
```

This is a suitable form of covenant to be used by individuals covenanting to a charity. Note that (a) the covenant payments can only be dated to start on or after the date of signing the deed (b) all deletions should be initialed (c) this is a form of 'gross' covenant. A 'net' form would make payments out of 'income net of tax at the standard rate'.

Administration

In order to recover tax on covenanted donations, the charity should apply to the Inland Revenue Claims Branch, Charity Division. Many companies and charities use the services of the Charities Aid Foundation (CAF) to administer covenants. (See Appendix, Useful Organisations).

Gift Aid - Companies

A company can also use Gift Aid to make one-off gifts to charities in a tax efficient manner. Companies making Gift Aid payments must be resident in the U.K. The company deducts basic rate income tax when it makes a payment to the charity and pays the tax over to the Inland Revenue. The charity claims the tax back from the Inland Revenue. The gross amount of the payment is allowed as a deduction against the company's profits for Corporation Tax purposes.

Gift Aid - Individuals

Single gifts or cash to charities by individuals out of their taxable earnings, of not less than £250 (net of standard rate tax) per gift and without any upper limit, have the same tax attributes as covenanted donations. Donors must duly notify the Inland Revenue on the relevant tax form, which can be completed after the date of the gift.

Other tax-free gifts

Certain other limited payments count as business expenses and are therefore deductible in calculating tax. In outline these are donations for technical education conducted at approved institutes; for approved research; and smallish gifts to local charities under Extra-Statutory concession B7 through the local Inspector of Taxes. In each case the education, research or projects must be related to the trade of the business.

Value Added Tax (VAT)

There is no general relief for charities, but there are a number of special reliefs.

Exempt supplies include:

(1) The provision of education or research by educational establishments and professional training by charities;
(2) Providing care, treatment or instructions to promote the welfare of elderly, sick, distressed or disabled persons;
(3) Goods and services closely linked to the protection of children and young persons;

(4) Goods and services provided by a charity in connection with a one-off fundraising event.

Zero rated supplies

(1) Sales of talking books for the blind and handicapped and wireless sets for the blind (e.g. Royal National Institute for the Blind);
(2) Sales of equipment for the relief of the chronically sick and disabled;
(3) The sale of donated goods in charity shops;
(4) The export of goods by a charity.

NB. Generally, none of these exempt or zero rated supplies must be supplied other than by or for charities or public bodies.

Generally, charities with taxable supplies (i.e. goods and services supplied by them for which they charge) of more than £37,600 a year (1993-1994 figure) (towards which zero rated, but not exempt, supplies count) must register for VAT. If taxable supplies exceed £37,600 the charity must notify Customs & Excise within 30 days of the end of the month within which the limit is breached. Those with less have neither to register nor charge VAT on taxable supplies. Each branch of a charity may be able to be treated as a separate entity.

NB. 1 This is a complex technical subject. Further information is available from your local VAT Inspector at Customs and Excise or from the National Council for Voluntary Organisations (NCVO) (which supplies an excellent, detailed guide "Charities' Primary Guide to VAT" - see Appendix, Further Reading) or Charities Tax Reform Group.

NB. 2 Where members of a charity pay subscriptions and receive benefits in return, there is both a general tax danger and a VAT danger. Take advice.

Inheritance Tax (IT)

Generally: until 1975 there was Estate Duty. This was replaced by Capital Transfer Tax. From 18 March 1986 this was replaced by Inheritance Tax. Like its predecessors, it is formidably complex, so beware. Where chargeable, the tax is at a flat rate of 40% (after 14 March 1988). The good news is that, as far as charities are concerned, IT is relatively simple and very generous. These are the key points:

Charities and tax relief

(1) Gifts of any amount, whether made in life or on death, are completely exempt from IT. That is to say, the assets gifted are taken completely out of the giver's estate for IT purposes, and of course the charity pays nothing.
(2) If, however, the gift is complicated by having conditions attached to it, or is postponed in effect, or is only for a limited period, or entitles the giver to retain some benefit out of the gift, or comes out of trust, then some IT may well be payable and advice should be taken from a solicitor or accountant.

Capital Gains Tax (CGT)

The charity: charities pay no CGT on receipt of gifts or on sale of their own assets (subject to anti-abuse measures - see Loss of Tax Exemptions).

The giver: If a taxpayer gives assets to a charity then he or she will not be liable for any CGT. There is no limit to this exemption.

Give-As-You-Earn (GAYE) , or Payroll Giving Tax Relief

As from 5 April 1987 employees were able to give up to £120 a year to charity out of their salaries at source. The limit was increased to £900 a year on 6 April 1993.

To take advantage of this revolutionary opportunity (which too few are still aware of) the employer needs to agree to administer the scheme with an approved collecting and distributing agent. (Advice can be given by the Payroll Services Unit of the Charities Aid Foundation - see Appendix, Useful Organisations.)

Non-residence

A donor who is not resident in the UK for tax purposes and who wants to make tax privileged payments to a UK charity will probably have to make that gift to a co-operative intermediate charity in his or her country of residence to obtain whatever tax concessions are available there for charitable donations. In this, as in so many other matters concerning tax, professional guidance is likely to be essential.

Charitable Status

NB. Definition of charity: Note that the Taxes Act exemption for charities (see S.506 Taxes Act 1988) only extends to charities 'established' here. That generally means those governed from, or mainly resident, here.

Loss of tax exemptions - generally

The Inland Revenue has long been worried about two developments. First, the major abuse by a few individuals of charity tax exemptions, often involving avoidance of corporation tax by covenanting profits to a 'captive' charity, sometimes with 'escape' payments by it abroad. The second main area of concern relates to inactive trustees - who allow their charitable funds to accumulate idly from year to year.

As a result, some unhappily complicated new provisions were enacted in 1986 which now appear as Sections 505, 506 and Schedule 20 to the Taxes Act 1988. They are far reaching, and if a charity falls foul of them it will lose its tax exemptions.

Most gifts are free of tax

Categories of charity with nothing to worry about

Charities and tax relief

(1) Charities whose relevant Income and Gains (RIGs) for the year concerned are less than £10,000. RIGs include covenanted income, dividends, interest, capital gains, rents, one-off gifts by companies, Gift Aid gifts, gifts from other charities and profits of any trade carried on by the charity.

(2) Charities which:

(a) Make no non-qualifying investments or loans (mainly those to private companies for which approval has not been obtained from the Inland Revenue), and

(b) Do not incur any non-qualifying expenditure (i.e. do not misapply their funds as by making non-charitable payments or donations).

(3) Surprisingly, even charities which cannot bring themselves within (2) above (because they have misspent funds) will nonetheless keep their tax exemptions if their proper (that is to say qualifying) charitable expenditure (on grants, expenses incurred in running the charity and finance charges) exceed their RIGs for the year.

Conclusion

Only those charities not able to bring themselves within one or other of these categories in any year will be in danger of losing tax relief. They will almost certainly need professional advice.

NB1. Where charities lose their tax exemptions the trustees or directors may be personally liable if improper expenditures are the cause.

NB2. Definition of the above terms (such as RIGs and qualifying expenditure) are to be found in Sections 505, 506 and Schedule 20 of the Taxes Act 1988.

NB3. The free Inland Revenue booklet Tax Relief for charities (IR.75) is very helpful (See Appendix, Further Reading).

NB4. Special clearance is needed not only for certain loans and investments but also for overseas grants.

NB5. Qualifying expenditure (see previous page) also includes commitments incurred (even where there may not have been an actual payment in the period of account), of a non-contractual, as well as a contractual, nature.

Rates - Non-Domestic Property

Non- domestic property is subject to the rating system introduced by the Local Government Finance Act 1988. This introduced three categories of rate relief:

a) Where the property is used for religious worship (a certificate is needed except in respect of the Church of England or the Church in Wales) or for the disabled (training or welfare or other facilities) there is complete exemption from rates.

b) Where the property is "wholly or mainly used for charitable purposes" (which includes premises so used by a charity for the sale of donated goods) mandatory 80% relief is available. The local council also has discretion to relieve the charity of the remaining 20% rate burden.

c) Where the property is wholly or mainly used by a not-for-profit recreational organisation or occupied by a not-for-profit philanthropic, social welfare, educational, religious, scientific, literary or fine arts organisation, the council has complete discretion to relieve the organisation from rates.

Council Tax - Domestic Property

The Council Tax was introduced by the Local Government Finance Act 1992 and became effective from 1st April 1993. It replaced the short-lived and inequitable Poll Tax. It is essentially a property-based tax and will catch charitable and voluntary domestic property if they can be defined as "dwellings".

The Council Tax has two elements, a 50% property part and a 50% personal part. The tax is complicated with seventeen categories of property entitled to exemption (mostly unoccupied ones) and thirteen groups of people who can be 'disregarded' in assessing liability (given that the assumption is that each household will comprise an average of two adults, with a 25% discount allowable where there is only one and 50% if there are none). Exempt dwellings include, for example, hospitals and halls of residence. 'Disregarded' groups include, for example, severely mentally impaired people, long stay hospital patients, students, patients in nursing and residential care homes and care workers. Charities should seek specific advice on Council Tax liability from the local authority or a relevant advice giving body (see Appendix, Useful Organisations).

Halfway-house charities

Individuals or companies can often be encouraged to give more to charity if they set up their own 'halfway-house charity'. As has been already remarked, one of the most pleasurable motives for many individuals and companies in giving to charity is the thought that hard-earned income is to be diverted from the Inland Revenue in the form of tax to a charity in the form of a gift! But this can only happen if one is willing to make a Gift Aid gift, or commit oneself to giving to one particular charity for more than three years.

Few people or companies want to be so single-minded but would much rather spread their money around from year to year as they think it can be best utilised. The halfway-house charity provides a solution. The key is to set up a simple charitable trust whose objects include all the four charitable categories. Any money received by that charity can then be spent by the trustees on any charitable purpose.

The constitution of the trust can be relatively simple, and provide maximum scope for the trustees as regards power of investment and decision making. Here another advantage accrues. Without a halfway-house charity one can only make tax exempt covenants to an 'established' charity. With the halfway-house charity, however, the trustees can give 'for charitable purposes'. This would allow them for example to make a grant to a non-charity or an individual so long as it was clearly earmarked, accepted and spent by that non-charity or individual for a charitable project or purpose. This can be simply arranged in advance with the donor.

Charitable Status

Another advantage of the halfway house charity is that the person setting it up can be a trustee with his or her 'nearest and dearest', although the Charity Commission likes at least one trustee from outside the immediate family of the founder. Where a company sets up a charity, however, it is usually perfectly satisfactory to confine trustees to directors and/or shareholders and/or employees.

Having established a halfway house charity the founder, whether company or individual, executes a coventional four year covenant in favour of the new halfway-house charity and/ or makes Gift Aid donations. Each year the trustees of the charity recover the tax and decide with full flexibility how to dole out this charitable money.

Appendix 1

Useful Organisations

ACENVO

The Association of Chief Executive Officers of National Voluntary Organisations. It runs training and induction programmes and co-ordinates a network for members to share expertise.

ACENVO, High Brow, Harrow Park, Harrow on the Hill, Middlesex HA1 3JE. Telephone: 081-869 1214.

Action: Employees in the Community

Through its network of 12 regional offices, Action: Employees in the Community (formerly known as Action Resource Centre) transfers business skills and resources to community organisations, to help them deal more effectively with inner city problems.
It promotes and arranges secondments from companies and other employing bodies to community organisations.

Head office: 8 Stratton St, London W1X 5FD Telephone: 071-629 2209.

Arts Council of Great Britain

The Arts Council is the main channel set up to distribute government money for the arts. Its Information Unit can provide newly updated model constitutions for arts groups.

Information Unit, *Arts Council of Great Britain*, 14 Great Peter Street, London SW1P 3NQ. Telephone: 071-333 0100.

Association for Business Sponsorship of the Arts (ABSA)

Charitable Status

ABSA is the national organisation promoting business sponsorship of the arts. It has published the Arthur Andersen Tax Guide and provides free leaflets explaining tax rules. They can also give advice on the tax problems of sponsorship.

Association for Business Sponsorship for the Arts, Nutmeg House, 60 Gainsford Street, London SE1 2NY. Telephone: 071-378 8143.

Association of Charitable Foundations

A membership body for grant-making trusts to promote good practice and encourage philanthropic giving.

Association of Charitable Foundations, 52-54 High Holborn, London WC1V 6RL. Telephone: 071-404 1338.

The Association of Charity Officers

This association liaises between charities in the welfare and social services field. It provides information and advice to members and makes representations to Government and others on the effects of legislation on welfare charities.

The Association of Charity Officers, c/o RICS Benevolent Fund Ltd., Tavistock House North, Tavistock Square, London WC1H 9RJ. Telephone: 071-387 0578.

Association of Community Trusts and Foundations (ACTAF)

ACTAF promotes the formation of new community trusts to raise and distribute money locally, and provides advice and support to existing community trusts.

Association of Community Trusts and Foundations, 52-54 High Holborn, London WC1V 6RL. Telephone: 071-831 0033.

Association of Landowning Charities

The principal object of this association is to provide in respect of the investment land of charities, a similar service to that provided on other matters by the Legislation-Monitoring Service for Charities (see below). It also facilitates the exchange of views and information between landed charities on matters which affect their real property, both urban and rural.

Correspondence address: Helen Donoghue, *Association of Landowning Charities*, 12 Little College Street, London SW1P 3SH. Telephone: 071-222 1265.

Bradford Disaster Fund

This fund can provide general information concerning sudden major disasters.

Legal matters: Hammond Suddards Research, Salt Mill, Victoria Rd, Salaire, Shipley BD153LD. Telephone: 0274 588028.
Human/crisis issue: Michael Stewart/Peter Hodgkinson, Centre for Crisis Psychology, 25 Harper Grove, Sutton-in-Craven, West Yorkshire BD20 7JN. Telephone: 0535 35446.

Business in the Community

Business in the Community is a national partnership of 300 companies, central and local government, the voluntary sector and trade unions. It promotes greater involvement of all in the community by developing and publicising schemes towards the creation of jobs, and promotes corporate responsibility. It administers the Per Cent Club, a group of leading companies which have committed themselves to a level of community contributions related to profits or dividends.

Business in the Community, 8 Stratton St, London W1X 5FD Telephone: 071-629 1600.

The Charities Aid Foundation (CAF)

This charity was set up in 1924 to encourage and promote the flow of funds to charity. Advice is available on many aspects of charitable giving and fundraising such as taxation and charity

law and up-to-date information on grant-making trusts. CAF also provides a covenant service for individuals and companies which ensures that the maximum advantage is taken of tax concessions without any charge to the donor. They have facilities for setting up trusts and settlements and can act as guardian of capital transferred for charitable use. Additionally CAF operates a computerised covenant administration service for charities. Biennially they publish the invaluable Directory of Grant Making Trusts and each year a survey of the funding of the charity sector entitled Charity Trends.
They operate the payroll giving scheme Give As You Earn.

Charities Aid Foundation, 48 Pembury Road, Tonbridge, Kent, TN9 2JD. Telephone: 0732 771333.

Charities Advisory Trust (CAT)

CAT provides advice and training on all aspects of charity trading and shops including the requirements to establish a separate trading company and when this might be appropriate.

Charities Advisory Trust, Radius Works, Back Lane, London NW3 1HL. Telephone: 071-794 9835.

Charities Branch - Department of Finance and Personnel

Organisations wishing to claim charitable privileges and located in Northern Ireland should contact this department for advice. There is no register of Northern Ireland Charities.

Charities Branch, Department of Finance and Personnel. Rating Division, Londonderry House, 21-27 Chichester Street, Belfast BT1 4JJ. Telephone: 0232 234898.

Charities Effectiveness Review Trust (CERT)

This charity provides management audits within the voluntary sector. Its board of management includes the leaders of a number of national agencies and its panel of consultants is mainly comprised of staff members of national organisations.

Charities Effectiveness Review Trust, 114-118 Southampton Row, London WC1B 5AA. Telephone: 071-831 7798.

Charities Evaluation Services (CES)

CES offers advice and information on evaluation to the voluntary sector and training courses in self-evaluation. It undertakes evaluation consultancies.

Charities Evaluation Services, 1 Motley Avenue, Christina Street, London EC2A 4SU. Telephone: 071-613 1202

Charities Official Investment Fund and Charities Deposit Fund

The Charities Official Investment Fund is a long term, unit trust fund in which charities may invest through the Official Custodian for Charities (see below).
The Charities Deposit Fund alternatively, is a short term, cash investment fund which may be directly approached by individual charities wanting to invest cash sums.

Charities Official Investment Fund and Charities Deposit Fund, St Alphage House, Fore Street, London EC2Y 5AQ. Telephone: 071-588 1815.

Charities Tax Reform Group (CTRG)

CTRG is a campaigning organisation whose principal objective is to seek VAT and tax reforms for charities. It is concerned with improvements in the wider fiscal climate for charities and also with charity law reform issues particularly as these can have an impact on taxation policy.

Charities Tax Reform Group, 12 Little College Street, London SW1P 3SH. Telephone: 071-222 1265.

The Charity Commission for England and Wales

The Charities Act 1960 describes the general function of the Charity Commission as 'promoting the effective use of charitable resources by encouraging the development of better methods of administration, by giving charities trustees information or advice on any matter affecting the charity and by investigating and checking abuses'. The specific functions of the Charity Commission are exercised more frequently than these general functions. We shall only describe the more important functions briefly. For fuller information consult their leaflets listed under Further Reading.

The Commission produces an annual report which is an invaluable public guide to its recent actions and can be obtained from HMSO. The staff is split between three offices (London, Liverpool and Taunton). Currently there are three full-time and two part-time Commissioners, a number of Deputy and Assistant Commissioners.

Throughout this book we have stressed the importance of consulting the Charity Commission on whether or not a draft constitution (governing instrument) is charitable. If the Commission is satisfied that the organisation will be exclusively charitable in its action, they will often offer free advice on how its governing instrument may be varied to declare purposes which are exclusively charitable. You can request an interview if you think this would help in this process. The Commission now publishes a range of model constitutions which charities can adapt for their own use.

Many of the other specific functions of the Charity Commission are described in Chapter Six. The remit of the Commission extends to England and Wales only. There is no equivalent body for Scotland or Northern Ireland.

Southern Office: *Charity Commission*, St Alban's House, 57-60 Haymarket, London SW1Y 4QX. Telephone: 071-210 3000.
Northern Office: Graeme House, Derby Square, Liverpool L2 7SB. Telephone: 051-227 3191.
Taunton Office: Woodfield House, Tangier, Taunton, Somerset TA1 4BL. Telephone: 0823-345000.

Official Custodian for Charities

The Official Custodian can be asked to act as a custodian trustee to ensure safekeeping of land and property owned by a charity.

Official Custodian for Charities, Charity Commission, St Alban's House, 57-60 Haymarket, London SW1Y 4QX. Telephone: 071-210 3000.

Register of Charities

The Charity Commission maintains a Register of Charities which the public may consult. As well as being filed alphabetically and by area, the slips are filed by type of charities, thus allowing a reader to look up the purposes of various charities and learn how to contact them, and sometimes their approximate income. This is useful both when drawing up an objects clause and when fundraising.
Complete indexes are kept at the offices of the Charity Commission. Most local authorities keep registers of their local charities. For further information contact the Charity Commission or your local authority.

Copies of governing instruments and the accounts of charities may be obtained by applying to the Central Register of Charities in London, Liverpool or Taunton. A charge is made to cover photocopying costs.

Charity Finance Directors' Group

An organisation for financial directors which organises seminars on financial and accounting matters.
Charity Finance Directors' Group, c/o Barnardo's, Tanners Lane, Barkingside, Essex IG6 1QG. Telephone: 081-550 8822.

The Charity Forum

A network for people in the charity sector. There is a programme of talks and events.

The Charity Forum, 60 Laurel Avenue, Potters Bar, Herts EN6 2SB. Telephone: 0707-662448.

Civic Trust

This charity was founded in 1957 to improve and regenerate the environment in places where people live and work. Its aim is to uphold high standards of environmental quality. Active at both a national and local level. Groups committed to improving a local environment can register with the Civic Trust. Such groups as local historical associations and conservation societies can obtain a model charitable constitution and guidance in registering as a charity.

Civic Trust, 17 Carlton House Terrace, London SW1Y 5AW. Telephone: 071-930 0914.

Commission for Racial Equality (CRE)

Charitable Status

On occasions the Legal Advisors of the CRE are able to offer advice to relevant organisations wishing to register as charities.

Commission for Racial Equality, Elliot House, 10-12 Allington Street, London SW1E 5EH. Telephone: 071-828 7022.

Community Matters

Community Matters, formerly known as the National Federation of Community Organisations, represents the interests of local community organisations and offers information, advice and practical help to local community groups. They provide information sheets, and advice on legal, constitutional, management and financial matters. They can provide on request, a model constitution suitable for use by local community groups.

Community Matters, 8/9 Upper Street, London N1 0PQ. Telephone: 071-226 0189.

The Council for Charitable Support

The Council for Charitable Support brings together people who work in or with the voluntary sector and who have an interest in raising the level of support for charities in the UK. It disseminates proposals and initiatives benefiting charities and encourages collaboration and consultation to address newly identified problems or opportunities.

The Council for Charitable Support, 48 Pembury Rd, Tonbridge, Kent TN9 2JD Telephone: 0732 771333.

Directory of Social Change

The Directory of Social Change is an educational charity. It is the leading publisher of grant guides, advisory handbooks and information leaflets which give practical information and advice to those running charities and working in the voluntary sector. These include the *Guide to Grants for Individuals in Need,*

A Guide to the Major Trusts vols 1 & 2 and *A Guide to Company Giving*.
It also runs a range of training courses and seminars in fund-raising, financial management and communications and arranges conferences on particular issues of current interest.
A full booklist and details of current training courses are available on request.

The Directory of Social Change, Radius Works, Back Lane, London NW3 1HL. Telephone: 071-435 8171 (courses) 071-284 4364 (books).

Ethical Investment Research Service (EIRIS)

EIRIS is an independent research organisation which provides services to a variety of groups including charities. It will provide information to enable organisations to use non-financial criteria when making investment decisions. Charges made will vary according to the value of the portfolio.

Ethical Investment Research Services (EIRIS), 401 Bondway Business Centre, 71 Bondway, London SW8 1SQ. Telephone: 071-735 1351.

Inland Revenue Claims Branch

The Charity Division of the Claims Branch considers claims for tax exemption under Section 505 (1) of the Income Corporation Taxes Act 1988. It will also advise promoters of charities during setting-up procedures especially if the applicant falls outside the remit of the Charity Commission. For enquiries regarding the VAT position of charities, you should contact your local VAT office, who will advise you and can provide leaflets. Their address will be in the phone book under Customs and Excise.

England, Wales and Northern Ireland. Charities Division, Inland Revenue Claims Branch, St John's House, Merson Road, Merseyside, L69 9BB. Telephone: 051-922 6363.
Scotland. Charities Division, Inland Revenue Claims Branch, Trinity Park House, South Trinity Road, Edinburgh EH3 3SD. Telephone: 031-522 6255.

Institute of Charity Fundraising Managers (ICFM)

Charitable Status

The Institute was established in 1983 to improve standards of performance and ethical practice in charity fundraising. Membership is open to individuals only at an annual fee of £30, and all members must abide by their strict code of practice regarding fundraising ethics. Services offered to members include a quarterly newsletter, advice from experts in the field and the exchange of information amongst members. The Institute publishes specialist codes of practice and runs a reference library.
The ICFM Trust is an educational trust given charitable status in 1984, and provides education and training in charity fundraising.

The *Institute of Charity Fundraising Managers*, 1 Market Towers, Nine Elms Lane, London SW8 5NQ. Telephone: 071-627 3436.

The InterChange Trust

The Interchange Trust provides legal advice for the voluntary sector, on charitable registration, company formation, constitutions, employment and management committee problems and the responsibilities and liabilities of trustees. The Trust is a registerered charity and keeps all costs to a minimum. Initial meetings and some of the services are free of charge.
It also runs courses at InterChange Studios for community organisations and arts groups on management skills, marketing and publicity, funding and finance, legal responsibilies, training and counselling and staff development. In-house training and consultancy are also offered, eg. for management committees on their role and responsibilities.

InterChange Trust, InterChange Studios, Dalby Street, Kentish Town, London NW5 3NQ. Telephone: 071-267 9421. InterChange Training also has a direct line/answerphone: 071-267 5220.

Legislation Monitoring Service for Charities

Set up in 1978 this service draws the attention of members to current legislation and proposed legislation as it may affect charities. A parallel European information service is being developed.

Legislation Monitoring Service for Charities, 12 Little College Street, London SW1P 3SH. Telephone: 071-222 1265.

National Association of Community Relations Councils

This association represents 100 Community Relations Councils and can give information to voluntary organisations and charities on community relations.

National Association of Community Relations Councils, 8-16 Coronet Street, London N1 6HD. Telephone: 071-739 6658.

National Association of Councils for Voluntary Service

This association has a membership of organisations which function to support and advise local charities. It provides information and advice to local Councils of Voluntary Service and similar bodies.

National Association of Councils of Voluntary Service, 3rd Floor, Arundel Court, 177 Arundel Street, Sheffield S1 2NU. Telephone: 0742 786636.

National Council for Voluntary Organisations (NCVO)

Amongst the services offered by the NCVO to voluntary organisations is advice on legal matters. Its Legal Department is available to help existing or potential organisations on legal matters from employment to lotteries and gaming. They are particularly well informed on charity law and the registration of charities. Its Trustee Development Unit provides advice on trustee matters and circulates information on training events.

Its international department can advise on European matters. Various departments within the Council reproduce bulletins, journals and newsletters.

National Council for Voluntary Organisations, Regent's Wharf, 8 All Saints Street, London N1 9RL. Telephone: 071-713 6161.

National Federation of Housing Associations

The National Federation is the central organisation for advising and co-ordinating housing associations and making representations on their behalf.

Charitable Status

The Federation will undertake the registration of housing associations which includes the provision of model rules. Their model H.13 1977 establishes a housing association as an Industrial and Provident Society having charitable status.

National Federation of Housing Associations, 175 Grays Inn Road, London WC1X 8UP. Telephone: 071-278 6571.

Northern Ireland Council of Voluntary Action

An organisation for the Northern Ireland voluntary sector fulfilling a similar function to the National Council for Voluntary Organisations.

Northern Ireland Council of Voluntary Action, 127 Ormeau Road, Belfast BT7 1SH. Telephone: 0232-321224

Registry of Friendly Societies

This Registry is responsible both for Friendly Societies and for Industrial and Provident Societies. Amongst its major functions are to register the rules of new societies and changes made to them and to maintain a public record of societies and their annual returns.

Registry of Friendly Societies, 15-17 Great Marlborough Street, London W1V 2QX. Telephone: 071-437 9992.

Scottish Council for Voluntary Organisations (SCVO)

An organisation for the Scottish voluntary sector fulfilling a similar function to the National Council for Voluntary Organisations.

SCVO, 18-19 Claremont Crescent, Edinburgh EH7 4QD. Telephone: 031-556 3882.

Voluntary Services Unit (VSU)

The VSU is the department within the Home Office responsible for the voluntary sector and for co-ordinating government policy towards the voluntary sector.
Voluntary Services Unit, Home Office, 50 Queen Anne's Gate, London SW1H 9AT. Telephone: 071-273 2146.

The Volunteer Centre UK

The Volunteer Centre UK is the national agency promoting volunteering. It provides information, training courses and specialist advice on many issues, including voluntary work by unemployed people and links between the business sector and volunteers. It also publishes a wide range of publications.

The Volunteer Centre UK, 29 Lower Kings Road, Berkhamsted, Hertfordshire HP4 2AB. Telephone 04428 73311.

Wales Council for Voluntary Action

An organisation for the Welsh voluntary sector fulfilling a similar function to the National Council for Voluntary Organisations.

Wales Council for Voluntary Action, Llys Ifor, Crescent Road, Caerffili CF8 1XL. Telephone: 0222-869224.

Appendix 2

Further reading

Accountancy Services for Voluntary Organisations

W Howard Press. NVCO, 1992.
£6.00 ISBN 0 7199 13675

Arts Funding Guide

Anne-Marie Doulton. Directory of Social Change, 1994.
£15.95 ISBN 1 873860 31 5

A Business Briefing: Charities

Institute of Chartered Accountants in England and Wales, 1992.
£25.00 ISBN 1 85355 3476
Available from Accountancy Books, PO Box 620, Central Milton Keynes MK9 2JX.

The Central Government Grants Guide

Anne-Marie Doulton. Directory of Social Change, 1993.
£12.95 ISBN 0 907164 93 5

Charitable Deductions (Approved Schemes) Regs 1986

HMSO, 1986.
£1.40 ISBN 011 068211 4

Charities: An Auditing Guideline

Institute of Chartered Accountants in England and Wales, 1981.
£4.00 ISBN 0 85291 5128
Available from Accountancy Books, PO Box 620, Central Milton Keynes MK9 2JX.

Charities: Constitutional Forms and Liabilities of Trustees

NCVO Guidance Note no. 2, 1981.
Free with A4 SAE.

The Charities Manual

Tolley.
£80 (plus a charge for any subsequent up-dates)
Available from Tolley Publishing Company, Tolley House, 2 Addiscombe Rd, Croydon, Surrey CR9 5AS.

Charities: The New Law The Charities Act 1992

Fiona Middleton and Stephen Lloyd. Jordan and Sons, 1992.
£19.95 ISBN 0 85308 140 9
Available from the Directory of Social Change.

Charity

Charities Aid Foundation.
Monthly magazine. £36 yearly subscription.

Charity Accounting

Elizabeth Cairns. Sweet and Maxwell, 1993.
£45 ISBN 0421 438 10X
Available from Sweet and Maxwell, North Way, Andover, Hants SP10 5BE.

Charity Investment - Law and Practice

Fiona Middleton and Andrew Phillips
Charities Aid Foundation

Charity Package

Inland Revenue.
Available free of charge to registered charity treasurers and trustees from the Inland Revenue Charity Division (051-922 6363).

Charity Trends

Charities Aid Foundation, 1993.
£20 ISBN 0 904757 96 X

Committees Workpack

Scottish Council for Voluntary Organisations (SCVO), 1986.
£3.50 ISBN 0 903589 88 5

Charitable Status

The Complete Fundraising Handbook

Sam Clarke. Directory of Social Change, 1993.
£12.95 ISBN 1 873860 21 8

Constitutions Workpack

Scottish Council for Voluntary Organisations (SCVO), 1986.
£7.50 ISBN 0 903589 87 7

Corporate Citizen

Directory of Social Change.
Quarterly journal (Jan, April, July and Oct). £30 a year for voluntary organisations, £55 for others.

Craigmyle Guide to Charitable Giving and Taxation

Craigmyle and Co.
Annually up-dated, looseleaf guide available from Craigmyle & Co., The Grove, Harpenden, Herts AL5 1AH.
£37.50 for initial purchase plus up-dates, £15 a year thereafter for up-dates.

Croner's Management of Voluntary Organisations

Croner Publications
First year's subscription (incl. up-dates) £99.10 plus £4.55 postage
Renewal fee (revised annually) £54.60
Available from Croner Publications Ltd, Croner House, London Rd, Kingston-upon-Thames, KT2 6SR.

Directory of Grant Making Trusts

Charities Aid Foundation, 1993.
£50 plus £3.80 p&p ISBN 0 904757 74 9

Education Act 1989 Ch 39

HMSO.
30p ISBN 0 11 801293 2

Educational Grants Directory

Paul Brown and Dave Casson. Directory of Social Change, 1994.
£15.95 ISBN 1 873860 46 3

Equity and the Law of Trusts

Pettit. Butterworth,1993.
£28.95 ISBN 0406 027692
Available from Butterworth Publishers, Borough Green, Kent TN15 8PH.

Finding Funds - General Information on Funding for Voluntary Groups

S Haydon. NCVO, 1991.
£7.50 ISBN 0 7199 1329 6

Fundraising Consultants: Listing for Voluntary Organisations

W Howard Press. NCVO, 1992
£5.00 ISBN 0 7199 13373

Gift Aid: A Guide for Donors and Charities (ref IR 113)

Inland Revenue, 1990.
Available free from any Inland Revenue office

Giving to Charity: How businesses can get tax relief (ref IR64)

Inland Revenue, 1992.
Free leaflet available from any Inland Revenue office.

Grants from Europe

Anne Davison and Bill Seary. NCVO, 1993/4.
£9.95 ISBN 0 7199 1382 9.

A Guide to Company Giving

Mike Eastwood. Directory of Social Change, 1993.
£14.95 ISBN 0 907164 96 X

A Guide to Grants for Individuals in Need

Dave Casson and Paul Brown. Directory of Social Change, 1994.
£15.95 ISBN 1 873860 45 5

A Guide to the Major Trusts Volume 1

Andrew Farrow and Luke FitzHerbert. Directory of Social Change, 1993.
£14.95 ISBN 0 907164 95 1

A Guide to the Major Trusts Volume 2

Dave Casson, Mike Eastwood and Paul Brown. Directory of Social Change, 1993.
£14.95 ISBN 1 873860 20 X

Insurance Protection: A Guide for Voluntary Organisations

NCVO, 1992.
£5.00 ISBN 0 7199 13462

Law and Practice relating to Charities

Picarda. Butterworth, 1994.
Price not fixed. ISBN 0 406117 64 0.
Available from Butterworth Publishers, Borough Green, Kent TN15 8PH.

Law relating to Trusts and Trustees

Underhill. Butterworth, 1987 (with 1992 supplement).
£145 ISBN 0 406 40593 X
Available from Butterworth Publishers, Borough Green, Kent TN15 8PH.

The Law of Trusts

Riddall. Butterworth, 1992
£22.95 ISBN 0 406 518408
Available from Butterworth Publishers, Borough Green, Kent TN15 8PH.

Legal Issues for Voluntary Organisations: A Reading List

NCVO New edition due. Price and ISBN not confirmed.

Legal Responsibilities of Members of Committees of Unincorporated Charitable Organisations
NCVO Guidance note no 1, 1990.
Free with A4 SAE

The London Grants Guide
Lucy Stubbs. Directory of Social Change, 1992.
£12.50 ISBN 0 907164 85 4

The Major Companies Guide 1994
Dave Casson. Directory of Social Change, 1994.
£14.95 ISBN 01 873860 22 6

A Practical Guide to VAT for Charities
Kate Sayer. Directory of Social Change, 1992.
£9.95 ISBN 0 907164 99 4

Recreational Charities Act 1958 Ch17 UK
HMSO.
30p ISBN 0 11 801297 5

Report of the Charity Commissioners for England and Wales
HMSO, 1993. (Price not fixed)

Specimen Constitution for an Unincorporated Charitable Organisation Having a Membership
NCVO, 1990. £2.50

Specimen Deed of Charitable Trust
NCVO, 1990. £2.50

Specimen Memorandum and Articles of Association for a Charitable Company Limited by Guarantee
NCVO, 1985.
£5.00

Trust Monitor
Directory of Social Change
3 times a year information service (Feb, June and Oct) £25 a year.

Charitable Status

Tax Relief for Charities (ref IR75)
Inland Revenue,1987.
Free leaflet available from any Inland Revenue Office

Trusts and Trustees - Cases and Materials
Maudsley and Burn. Butterworth, 1990.
£30.95 ISBN 0 406 59211 X
Available from Butterworth Publishers, Borough Green, Kent TN15 8PH.

Tudor on Charities
Morris and Parker. Sweet & Maxwell, 1989 (with supplement)
£168 ISBN 0421 417 501
Available from Sweet & Maxwell, North Way, Andover, Hants SP10 5BE.

Value Added Tax (Charities and Aids for Handicapped persons) Order
HMSO, 1992.
65p ISBN 0 11 023628 9

What is a Charity? Charity Law and Formation of Charities
NCVO, 1992.
£2.50

The following explanatory leaflets are available free of charge from the Charity Commission. Send a large stamped self-addressed envelope to any of the Commissioners' offices with your order.

The Charity Commissioners: How they can help Charity Trustees
Responsibilities of Charity Trustees
Responsibilities of Charity Trustees - A Summary
Charities for the Relief of the Poor

Charities for the Relief of Sickness
Ex Gratia Payments by Charities
Political Activities by Charities
The Official Custodian for Charities' Land Holding Service
Investment of Charity Funds: Basic Principles
Investing Charity Cash
Official Custodian for Charities Common Investment Funds
The Relief of the Unemployed
The Promotion of Racial Harmony
Use of Church Halls for other Charitable Purposes
Fundraising and Charities
Starting a Charity
Charities Acts 1960 and 1985 Charity Accounts
Provision of Alcohol on Charity Premises
Charity Land
Charities and Local Authorities
Educational Charities
Trustee Investments Act 1961
Acquiring Land
Making a Scheme
Capital Expenditure by Charity Trustees
Extraordinary Repair Funds
Disaster Appeals - Attorney General's Guidelines
Payment of Charity Trustees
Small Charities: Alteration of Trusts, Transfer of Property, Expenditure of Capital
Central Register of Charities: Services Available
Investigating Charities
Registration of Religious Charites

Appendix 3

Index